ABOUT

Robert Barry is a sta
Education in Northe
chology, is a member of

‘Psychology, God and the New Physics’. This is his first book.
He lives with his wife and three children in Co. Down,
Northern Ireland.

“A major contribution to the debate on who or what we are and
where we might be going.” — **Irish News**

“Widely read, an impressive serendipity of references.” —
Journal of Beliefs and Values

“Deeply felt and interestingly presented . . . Barry is thoughtful,
intelligent, concerned.” — **Mensa International Journal**

“A useful way of integrating science, psychology and mysticism
into a theory of the evolution of consciousness.” — **Scientific &
Medical Network**

“Intriguing and challenging . . . sure to stretch the frontiers of the
mind of the reader.” — **County Down Spectator**

ACKNOWLEDGEMENTS

I wish to express my sincere thanks to the many people who assisted me in the ten years of research that went into this book.

I am particularly grateful to Karen Trew and Carol McGuinness of the Queen's University of Belfast, and to Helen Graham of Keele University for providing me with invaluable advice and guidance along the way.

Particular thanks must also go to Patricia Jamshidi, Deirdre McCullough, Anjam Khursheed, Robert Parry and Juliet Mabey for their very helpful suggestions and comments on earlier drafts.

To Professor Ken Brown and all the staff at the School of Psychology of the Queen's University of Belfast, where this research was undertaken, thanks for putting up with me over the years and for providing me with a great deal of support and encouragement.

Finally, a very special thank you to my wife, Valerie, whose support, understanding and occasional criticism I could not have done without.

A
THEORY
OF ALMOST
EVERYTHING

A
SCIENTIFIC AND RELIGIOUS
QUEST
FOR ULTIMATE ANSWERS

ROBERT BARRY

ONEWORLD
OXFORD

*To two people who lived not for themselves
but for others – my parents, Robert and Joyce.*

Oneworld Publications
(Sales and Editorial)
185 Banbury Road, Oxford, OX2 7AR
England

Oneworld Publications
(US Marketing Office)
PO Box 830, 21 Broadway
Rockport, MA 01966
USA

A Theory of Almost Everything
© Robert Barry 1993
First published in hardback 1993
Published in paperback 1996
Reprinted 1998

A CIP record for this book is available from the British Library

ISBN 1-85168-123-X

Printed and bound by WSOY, Finland

D ESIDERATA

Go placidly amid the noise and haste,
And remember what peace there may be in silence.
As far as possible without surrender be on good terms with
all persons.
Speak your truth quietly and clearly; and listen to others,
Even the dull and ignorant; they too have their story.

Avoid loud and aggressive persons,
They are vexatious to the spirit.
If you compare yourself with others, you may become vain
and bitter;
For always there will be greater and lesser persons than
yourself.
Enjoy your achievements as well as your plans.

Keep interested in your own career, however humble;
It is a real possession in the changing fortunes of time.
Exercise caution in your business affairs;
For the world is full of trickery.
But let this not blind you to what virtue there is;
Many persons strive for high ideals;
And everywhere life is full of heroism.

Be yourself. Especially do not feign affection.
Neither be cynical about love;

For in the face of all aridity and disenchantment
It is perennial as the grass.

Take kindly the counsel of the years,
Gracefully surrendering the things of youth.
Nurture strength of spirit to shield you in sudden misfortune,
But do not distress yourself with imaginings.
Many fears are born of fatigue and loneliness.
Beyond a wholesome discipline, be gentle with yourself.

You are a child of the universe,
No less than the trees and the stars;
You have a right to be here.
And whether or not it is clear to you,
No doubt the universe is unfolding as it should.

Therefore be at peace with God,
Whatever you conceive Him to be,
And whatever your labors and aspirations,
In the noisy confusion of life keep peace with your soul.

With all its sham, drudgery and broken dreams,
It is still a beautiful world.
Be careful. Strive to be happy.

> (*From a manuscript found in Old Saint Paul's
> Church, Baltimore, dated 1692*)

Contents
····················

Introduction 9

INTRODUCTION
....

After spending twelve years of his life writing a comprehensive textbook on psychology, William James, one of
the most famous psychologists of all time, declared that he
had grown tired of this 'nasty little subject' and that 'all one
cares to know lies outside it'.[1] He spent most of the rest of his
life studying religion and philosophy. Now I believe I understand why.

In 1979, I embarked on a degree course in psychology. I
hoped that, at the end of it, I would be much wiser, having
discovered a number of secrets about people and why they do
what they do. After thirteen years of studying psychology,
I'm certainly a lot older. If I'm any wiser, I believe it is
through being forced to search for answers outside this 'nasty
little subject'.

A new psychology, however, is beginning to emerge, and
will stretch the discipline beyond its present limits. This new
psychology is both transpersonal and holistic. Transpersonal,
in that it takes us beyond that narrow self towards which psychologists have in the past directed us, and holistic, in that it
embraces the entire cosmos in the recognition that everything is connected to everything else.

That is what this book is about. Based on ten years of
research, it attempts to take the reader beyond the philosophy
of 'self-fulfilment' and tries to provide a single framework for
understanding the many different realities that we experi-

ence. The latter aim represents a dream held by some modern physicists, such as Stephen Hawking, and by great thinkers in the past, such as Isaac Newton and Albert Einstein. I believe we are not far from realizing that dream, or at least coming as close to its realization as the limitations of the human mind will allow. As well as drawing on physics, I have also turned to religion for the missing piece of the jigsaw that science alone can never hope to complete, to provide a completely new theory of the self that links into scientific and religious views of reality.

Part I confronts the reader with the concept of the 'Selfish Universe'. This is the universe in which most of us presently live. It is a universe rife with social and psychological problems, stemming from an illusion of separateness and our attempt to establish an independent self in an interconnected world. The result is an unquenchable thirst for the fulfilment of the impossible. We search for causes, we search for self, we sink more deeply into self consciousness, and finally the self replaces God. In our attempt to separate and enthrone the self, we discover instead of the fulfilment that psychologists promised us, a feeling of emptiness and meaninglessness. The more we attempt to fulfil ourselves, the less fulfilled we become. The Selfish Universe is a universe without a soul – it has no common essence to hold all the 'independent' pieces together.

Part II examines the 'Physical Universe' – the universe that most of us associate with 'reality' (the world of objects that obey various 'laws of nature'). Our perception of reality, however, is undergoing a major transformation, as we begin to dispel the illusion of separateness. With the 'new physics' leading physicists to ask questions about consciousness (an area which was formerly left to psychologists), a scientific synthesis of physics and psychology is now a possibility. By extending the basic idea behind the Theory of Relativity, I attempt to demonstrate this possibility in a theory that brings together space, time and mind. This merger between elements of the fundamental sciences of physics and psychology may take us closer to the much-sought-after 'theory of everything', but it still leaves us in a spiritual vacuum.

Part III goes beyond the physical world and the world of the self, to a universe based on mysticism (a concept that implies awareness of an underlying unity in all things through ascension to a higher level of consciousness). It draws together a number of threads from the controversial New Age movement, and introduces a relatively new religion. This new religion is not only compatible with science, but also has the potential for unifying all the world's major religions. In the emerging synthesis of science and religion, new light is shed on many of our present-day problems, especially those relating to our feelings of worthlessness or meaninglessness. The 'Mystical Universe' offers us freedom from our illusion of separateness, and holds the answers to all our questions. Above all, it offers the sense of meaning that we so desperately seek.

PART ONE

······················

THE
SELFISH
UNIVERSE

THE
ILLUSION
OF SEPARATENESS

Everything is connected to everything else. Everything that any one of us does, no matter how trivial it seems, has some impact on the rest of the world, no matter how infinitesimal.

This is the message of the *New* Physics, the *New* Biology, the *New* Psychology, and the whole *New Age* Movement generally. In the terms of the *New* Mathematics of Chaos Theory, it is referred to as the *Butterfly Effect*. One of the leading proponents of this latest movement in mathematics, James Gleick, describes it as 'the notion that a butterfly stirring the air today in Peking can transform storm systems next month in New York'.

He quotes the following little poem as an example of the Butterfly Effect.

> For want of a nail, the shoe was lost;
> For want of a shoe, the horse was lost;
> For want of a horse, the rider was lost;
> For want of a rider, the battle was lost;
> For want of a battle, the kingdom was lost![1]

The New Age philosophy of interconnectedness is about to permeate our thinking on just about every subject. The already powerful influence of the Green Movement is just the beginning. Until this new philosophy takes over from the old fragmented view of the world, however, most of us continue to view it in a piecemeal fashion. We search in vain for independent causes or reasons to explain everything that happens in our lives. We fracture the world into small pieces, and create an illusion of separateness. Amongst the pieces, we frantically search for a separate self, in the hope that if we find it, we will be able to promote its welfare and achieve lasting happiness. But what is the result of this search? Instead of happiness, we find meaninglessness and emptiness.

THE SEARCH FOR CAUSES

I pick up the newspaper and read of yet another death on the roads. Another tragedy that touches on the lives of all who shared experiences with the victim. What caused this apparently needless loss of life? Well, in this case it's easy to see what happened – the person in the other car had been drinking and came around the corner on the wrong side of the road. Poor John hadn't a chance. But wait – is it as simple as that?

What if John hadn't been impeded in his journey by that slow-moving lorry that took him almost ten minutes to pass? Surely the lorry driver contributed in some way to his death? After all, if he hadn't been on the road at that time, then John wouldn't have arrived at that fatal corner at the exact moment when some fool decided to change lanes. What about the lorry driver's wife? Did she have a hand in it too? Didn't she talk him into returning home early that evening? Normally he wouldn't have been on that road at that particular time. In fact, he had just put off another delivery so that he could get home in time for his daughter's birthday party.

What if his daughter hadn't been born on that particular date? Yes, that might have saved John. What about all the events leading up to the birth of the lorry driver's daughter? His marriage. The marriages of his and his wife's parents. His very existence and all the factors leading up to that particular existence. These were all, in some way, instrumental in John's death.

But of course, this is getting a bit silly now. We can't really point the finger at an innocent lorry driver and his family. It was the other driver who caused it . . . and maybe the other driver's workmates, who bought all those drinks for him at lunch time. They did tell him that those last three gins were small ones, even though they were really doubles. Well, he deserved a celebration; after all, he'd been waiting almost seven years for that promotion. Does that mean that his bosses had some part in the accident? Or perhaps it was Mr Brown's early retirement, which made the promotion and consequent celebration possible? In fact, if Mr Brown hadn't sustained that back injury last year, he would never have retired so soon. And it was such a stupid incident that led to the injury. It isn't wise to make a wild swipe at a passing fly whilst precariously balanced on a step-ladder. However, such is life, and it's no use crying over it now. It would appear, then, that the fly in Mr Brown's living room has a lot to answer for.

And all the time John's wife is mourning the loss of a loving husband and father, and suffering from terrible feelings of guilt. If she hadn't asked John to drive over to her sister's house . . . she even told him to hurry back. It was obviously her fault that John was now dead, and would not be around to help shape the lives of his two sons and only daughter. His death would alter the future of the whole family. If only . . .

Clearly, John's death can be attributed to the actions of a lot of people and to a lot of chance occurrences. But what really killed John? The answer is – everything. Everything worked together in a certain way to produce a particular set of consequences. John's fatal accident was one of those consequences. And so it is with everything in life.

The search for causes is futile in an interconnected world. To ask what *causes* a cold is as meaningless as to ask what causes a flower. To ask what *caused* the latest virus is no different from asking what caused humanity. To ask what *causes* death is as meaningless as to ask what causes the rain. If a heart attack is the answer to the former, then a black cloud must be the answer to the latter. And are we any the wiser for such answers? Spinoza summed up the position, over 300 years ago:

> If a stone has fallen from some roof on somebody's head and killed him, they will demonstrate in this manner that the stone has fallen in order to kill the man. For if it did not fall for that purpose by the will of God, how could so many circumstances occur through chance (and a number often simultaneously do concur)? You will answer, perhaps, that the event happened because the wind blew and the man was passing that way. But, they will urge, why did the wind blow at that time, and why did the man pass that way precisely at that moment? If you again reply that the wind rose then because the sea on the preceding day began to be stormy, the weather hitherto having been calm, and that the man had been invited by a friend, they will urge again – because there is no end of questioning – But why was the sea agitated? Why was the man invited at that time? And so they will not cease from asking the causes of causes, until at last you fly to the will of God.[2]

Despite the interconnectedness of everything in our world, we continue to search for causes or reasons. We point the finger of blame at ourselves, at others, or at 'the system' when things go wrong. Yet we often take personal credit when things go right. Too often we forget about the contributions of others. We forget that what happens to us depends on much more than our own efforts. We forget that we depend on the trees and plants around us for oxygen. We forget that we are all interdependent parts of a much greater whole.

THE SEARCH FOR SELF

> He who does not know what the world is, does not know where he is. And he who does not know for what purpose the world exists, does not know who he is, nor what the world is. But he who has failed in any one of these things could not even say for what purpose he exists himself. What then dost thou think of him who avoids or seeks the praise of those who applaud, of men who know not either where they are or who they are?
>
> — *Marcus Aurelius*[3]

Who are you? What are you? Are you all that you think; all that you do; all that you feel; or all that you think you are? Who decides who or what you are? After all, if you were to ask different members of your family to provide as comprehensive a description of you as they could, they would all give different answers. If you were to ask a group of strangers to provide such a description after you had spent an hour talking to them, you would receive an even more diverse range of responses. So, who or what are you? Are you the average of all these responses? The sum of the most commonly agreed parts of these responses? What psychologists, or perhaps even astrologers, say you are? The you that you present to others (and if so, which others)? Or are you just the private you that is known to no one else – the one that your spouse doesn't understand (or is it the one that your employer doesn't fully appreciate)?

First, I would like to make it quite clear that I don't know who you are. Psychologists don't know who you are. Astrologers most certainly don't know who you are. Even you don't know who you are. And none of us know where you're going either. Do not despair, however. My point is that we have no need to concern ourselves with such matters. In fact, it may be better for us if we don't.

We are born into this world without any self-awareness. Young children make no distinction between themselves and the world around them.[4] Gradually, they learn to separate themselves from the world through the acquisition of concepts such as 'I', 'me' and 'mine'.[5] Parents and other responsible adults reinforce the notion of a separate self,[6] providing the child with an individual identity ('you are Lisa') and even a description in terms of perceived physical and personal characteristics ('you are beautiful/clever'). The child loses its innocence. The world, of which it was once an integral part, becomes a separate and threatening entity.

Rightly or wrongly, the search for self, once instilled in us through an acquired sense of separateness, becomes obsessive. We continually seek feedback from others on the 'type' of person we are. So cranks and charlatans queue up to tell us what sort of people we are and, more importantly with such an uncertain world surrounding us, to tell us what is going to happen in the future. All we have to do is drink a cup of tea, cut a pack of cards, fill in a personality test, tell somebody when and where we were born, or hold out a hand (provided we have some money in the other hand).

Does the following description seem familiar? Would you regard it as a fair description of you?

> You have a great need for other people to like and admire you. You have a tendency to be critical of yourself. You have a great deal of unused capacity which you have not turned to your advantage. While you have some personality weaknesses, you are generally able to compensate for them . . . Disciplined and self-controlled outside, you tend to be worrisome and insecure inside. At times you have serious doubts as to whether you have made the right decision or done the right thing. You prefer a certain amount of change and variety and become dissatisfied when hemmed in by restrictions and limitations.

The above is part of a 'personality sketch' based on extracts from an astrology book. Each of the sentences is a universally valid statement that could apply to just about anybody. The sketch was used by a psychologist to demonstrate just how gullible most of us are.[7]

In an experiment conducted over forty years ago, Bertram Forer gave his students a bogus personality test, which he pretended to mark. One week later, the students were presented with the 'results' of the test in the form of copies of the sketch with their names on (each student was given the same sketch and told that it was a description of him or her based on the test). They were then asked to indicate how effective the test had been and to rate the degree to which the personality description had revealed basic characteristics of their personality. Most of the students indicated that the test was either perfect or near perfect in describing them.

Like a scientist you search for evidence to help you to piece together the most important puzzle of all – the puzzle of

You. Unfortunately, the vast majority of the pieces of this puzzle are not very clear. The evidence relating to them keeps changing, as do the bias in your selection of evidence and your perception of the pieces. Everyone is therefore highly susceptible to the suggestions of others.

i) Self-Fulfilling Prophecy

In a situation where we are not sure of who or what we are, we accept the labels that others give to us, and we fulfil any prophecies that they care to make about us. If I am labelled 'a criminal', I will assume the role of 'criminal'. If I am labelled 'stupid', I will behave 'stupidly' and I will come to believe that I am 'stupid', irrespective of the accuracy of the original judgement. If I do not know who I am, and I am looking for myself, and someone tells me 'this is you', then I will gladly play the part they have given me.

The phenomenon of the 'self-fulfilling prophecy' has been demonstrated repeatedly by psychologists and sociologists. In a number of classroom experiments, schoolchildren have been selected at random and their teachers told that they would show 'remarkable gains in intellectual development' based on the results of bogus 'tests'. By the end of the school year, these children have shown significant gains on IQ test scores as a result of their teachers' expectations and attitudes towards them.[8]

It seems that the expectations of significant others (such as parents and teachers), once internalized, are eventually fulfilled. It has also been shown, for example, that parents' expectations will play an important part in determining the success or failure of their children in later life.[9]

The self-fulfilling prophecy helps to reinforce and perpetuate the social stereotypes of females, ethnic minorities, and

any other social group. Women, for example, have for genera-
tions behaved 'like women'. They were expected to stay at
home, look after the children, and to shun success outside the
role of care-giver/sex object. Until feminists began to force
people to question this stereotype, most women simply
conformed to it. Women were told they were not as intelligent as men and could never cope with the world (outside the
home) as well as men. That was the message they believed,
and that was the prophecy they fulfilled – until recently. Now
that the myth of 'male superiority' has been dispelled, females
consistently outperform males in educational attainment.

Jerry Lynch captures the essence of the self-fulfilling
prophecy in the following poem:

If you THINK you are beaten, you are.
If you THINK you dare not, you don't.
If you like to win, but THINK you can't,
It is almost certain you won't!

If you THINK you'll lose, you've lost,
For out in the world we find,
Success begins with a person's WILL –
It's all in the state of MIND.

If you THINK you're outclassed, you are.
You've got to THINK high to rise.
You've got to be sure of yourself before
You can ever win a prize.

Life's battles don't always go
To the stronger or faster one,
But sooner or later the one who wins
Is the one who THINKS he can![10]

ii) Self-Image

Since we don't realize that we can be whatever we want to be (a point I will return to later), our self-image is filled with a confused mixture of illusion, media hype, and dubious interpretations from social encounters.

It is bad enough that we have problems in defining who or what we are, but just to make matters worse, it appears that we are often uncertain about how we feel. Psychologists have demonstrated that our perceptions of our emotions are influenced by social circumstances. If we experience feelings of arousal, we may label them differently according to the situation. The same feelings may be labelled as 'sexual arousal' in the presence of an attractive member of the opposite sex; as 'anger' when those around us appear angry in response to some event; as 'fear' when all around us flee in apparent panic; or as 'grief' in response to a death. We search for external clues to help us to label what we feel internally.

In one experiment, designed to demonstrate this, students were given injections of epinephrine – a drug that produces side effects such as increased heart rate and flushing of the face. When left, afterwards, in the company of a person behaving in a euphoric manner, they reported feeling happy. Others, who were left in the company of someone behaving angrily, reported that they felt angry.[11] Differing sets of external clues, therefore, led to differing labels being given to the same physical experience.

It is not surprising that so many people turn to psychologists, psychiatrists or astrologers for some sort of consistent picture of themselves. Personality descriptions from 'those who know about such things' are clutched like life rafts in a stormy sea. It is a great pity that so many of these rafts turn out to be too flimsy to cope with even the slightest breeze.

iii) The Ideal Self

If we are not too sure of the person we are at present, then how much more difficult must it be to know what we would like to be in future? Fortunately, we have advertisers and other media people to help us to make up our minds. At a more local level, we have the most aggressive and verbose members of our community to tell us just how it should be.

Aside from the rules and regulations for behaviour imposed upon us democratically, or otherwise, there are 'norms' and 'ideals' that most of us try to follow in the absence of any clear internal guidelines. Most of these standards stem from our religion and upbringing. In the western world, however, norms and ideals are, to a large extent, defined (and constantly re-defined) by the media of television, films, newspapers, magazines, and so on. From these sources, we decide who we would like to be and who we should be.

From the soft drink advertisements, we know we should be young, slim, good-looking, tanned (if Caucasian), and without spots, glasses or wheelchairs. From certain newspapers, we discover that all females should have thirty-six-inch chests, that everybody is having sex with everybody else, or, if not, they are being raped. Happy marriages, happy families, and acts of kindness do not feature prominently. From magazines, we learn that by paying more attention to ourselves (and by spending some of our hard-earned or yet-to-be-earned cash) we can make ourselves young, good-looking, sexually desirable, and successful. 'Successful' usually means winning at something or making lots of money. So, once again, the doctrines of competition and materialism are reinforced. The promise of a 'better' way of life is held out to those who can look younger, lose weight, smell better, or defeat others in competition.

For those who really are young, the public image of their musical or sporting heroes is all-important. The young are even less certain of who they are, so they look around them for role models to imitate. If their latest hero wears torn jeans, then that is the way to dress. If their latest hero supports the Green movement, then it must be okay. If he uses drugs, then that too must be okay. The image portrayed by pop musicians, actors, actresses and sporting heroes is therefore of crucial importance in shaping the values and attitudes of the young. Such images act as models for uncertain and aspiring youth.

iv) Self-Esteem

Irrespective of the difficulty we experience in forming a clear image of the self and of the norms and ideals that we would like to pursue, we cannot help forming some sort of judgement of ourselves based on the discrepancy between what we think we are and what we think we should be. This evaluation of the self equates roughly with self-confidence and is referred to by psychologists as 'self-esteem'. Not surprisingly, it fluctuates even more than one's self-image. If we do not possess a clear and consistent image of the self, then it is obviously difficult to form a clear and consistent opinion of it. In addition to a fluctuating self-image, we have an ever-changing context in which to evaluate it.

William James pointed out the importance of our ideals and aspirations in determining self-esteem. The following passage is taken from his *Principles of Psychology*, which was written a century ago.

I, who for the time have staked my all on being a psychologist, am mortified if others know much more psychology than I, but I am content to wallow in the grossest ignorance of Greek. My deficiencies there give me no sense of personal humiliation at all. Had I 'pretensions' to be a linguist, it would have been just the reverse. So we have the paradox of a man shamed to death because he is only the second pugilist or the second oarsman in the world. That he is able to beat the whole population of the globe minus one is nothing; he has 'pitted' himself to beat that one; and as long as he doesn't do that nothing else counts. He is to his own regard as if he were not, indeed he *is* not.

Yonder puny fellow, however, whom everyone can beat, suffers no chagrin about it, for he has long ago abandoned the attempt to 'carry that line', as the merchants say, of self at all. With no attempt there can be no failure, no humiliation. So our self-feeling in this world depends entirely on what we *back* ourselves to be and do.[12]

Despite the elusiveness of the self we continue to search for it, and even though we do not know who or what we are, we attempt to evaluate the nebulous image of self that we have created. We fail to realize that the separate self is an illusion. We fail to realize that the self is an integral part of all around it, and as such cannot be defined independently. The self that searches for itself is in the position of the hand that attempts to grasp itself.

LOOKING AFTER NUMBER ONE

For whom do you do most in your life? Is it yourself? Your partner? Your children? Your neighbours? The elderly? The sick? The poor? The 750 million starving people in the world?[13] The 800 million who can neither read nor write?[14]

The philosophy of 'looking after number one' is often extended to include number one's family, but most of us do not lose too much sleep over the suffering of those we do not know. The attitude held by most of us is probably summed up well by Bob Geldof in his *Great Song of Indifference* – 'Nah, nah, nah' to the rest of the world. How much of your own life do you recognize in the following scenario?

Johnny Average reached across the side of the bed and switched off the alarm clock. Reluctantly, he dragged himself into an upright position and into his dressing gown and slippers.

'Time to get up, darling', he loudly informed his wife, Jill, for the 2,532nd time in their marriage. Receiving no reply from the limp body in the bed, he continued towards the adjoining rooms.

'Billy! Susie! Up for school!' Simultaneous groans arose from two of the other rooms.

Looking in the bathroom mirror, Johnny frowned at his thinning hair and spreading waistline. The hair tonic and all those one-calorie Cokes that he was drinking didn't seem to be helping much. If only he could afford a hairtransplant and a facelift . . .

'Susie! Billy! Get up this instant, or you'll be late!' The two children jumped out of their beds at the sound of their mother's voice. 'Johnny, how many times must I tell you not to leave the top off the toothpaste?'

'Sorry, dear. Your tea is on the table when you're ready. Do you want any toast?'

'No thanks! I'll be down in a minute.'

Johnny turned his attention to the television. Nothing exciting on the news. Just the usual Middle East crisis stuff, another bombing in Belfast, and another child abduction. Nothing that was going to affect him. Wait a minute, though. Here was something important.

'Oh no! That's all we needed!'

'What's happened?' asked Jill, fearfully, as she arrived from the bathroom.

'They've put up interest rates again. If this keeps up, we'll be struggling with the mortgage.'

'Well, we'll just have to tighten our belts a bit.'

'Tighten our belts!' exclaimed Johnny. 'What about all the credit card bills, and your new car?'

'Not now, Johnny. It's too early in the morning for all this. Anyway, I'm already late for work, and Billy and Susie still aren't ready for school. Go and hurry them up!'

Jill had a narrow escape on the way into the office. She only just managed to avoid boring old Mrs Chatterly on her way in from the car park. The last thing she wanted right now was to listen to her complaining about her rheumatism. She had just dropped the children off at school, and was still thinking about Billy's poor marks. He had dropped from seventh in his class to fifteenth within the past few months. She couldn't help thinking that his friendship with that new boy, Jimmy Underaverage, had something to do with it. It didn't matter if he failed his exams at the end of the year, but she didn't want Billy to be dragged down to his level.

Johnny wasn't so lucky. He got stuck in another traffic jam.

'What are all these people doing out in their cars, anyway?' he thought to himself. Surely some of them could take the bus, or walk? Too many people. That was the problem. Too many cars. Too much affluence. It never used to be like this.

The news on the radio interrupted his thoughts momentarily. Something about another earthquake in California. Boy! Was he glad that he didn't live there. Just then, he noticed the reason for the traffic jam up ahead. Another car accident. It looked pretty nasty too, even from that distance. He was glad now that he hadn't left the house ten minutes earlier. Well, at least he would have an excuse for his delay when he got to the office . . .

The illusion of separateness narrows our vision. It leads Johnny Average to care more for himself and his family than for anybody else in the world. It leads Jill Average to care more for herself and her family than for an old lady with rheumatism or for all the other young boys and girls who must fail their exams to ensure that the word 'pass' retains some meaning.

Jill and Johnny may both see themselves as caring individuals. After all, they care more for other family members sometimes than they do for themselves. There is nothing wrong with this expression of love for others within the family, provided it is also extended to others outside the family. Like the rest of us, however, their view of the world is egocentric. They fail to realize that they have merely extended the illusion of a separate self to the illusion of a separate family. They forget that we are all of one family. They appear unaware that we are all integral parts of a much greater whole. The result – five billion people competing with each other in service of self (or an extension of self in the form of family) instead of five billion people living as one and serving the whole.

THE MEANINGLESSNESS OF LIFE

It is useless, useless, said the Philosopher. Life is useless, all useless. You spend your life working, laboring, and what do you have to show for it? . . . I, the Philosopher, have been king over Israel in Jerusalem. I determined that I would examine and study all the things that are done in this world.

God has laid a miserable fate upon us. I have seen everything done in this world, and I tell you, it is all useless. It is like chasing the wind. . . . I decided to enjoy myself and find out what happiness is. But I found that this is useless too. I discovered that laughter is foolish, that pleasure does you no good. Driven on by my desire for wisdom, I decided to cheer myself up with wine and have a good time. I thought that this might be the best way that people can spend their short lives on earth.

I accomplished great things. I built myself houses and planted vineyards. I planted gardens and orchards, with all kinds of fruit trees in them; I dug ponds to irrigate them. I bought many slaves and there were slaves born in my household. I owned more livestock than anyone else in Jerusalem. I also piled up silver and gold from the royal treasuries of the lands I ruled. Men and women sang to entertain me, and I had all the women a man could want.

Yes, I was great, greater than anyone else who had ever lived in Jerusalem, and my wisdom never failed me. Anything I wanted I got. I did not deny myself any pleasure. I was proud of everything I had worked for, and all this was my reward. Then I thought about all I had done and how hard I had worked doing it, and I realized that it didn't mean a thing. It was like chasing the wind – of no use at all.

(Ecclesiastes 1.2–3; 1.12–14; 2.1–11)

These are the words of the philosopher, Ecclesiastes, in what is described by the Jewish Rabbi and author, Harold Kushner as the 'most dangerous book in the Bible',[15] because of the message of hopelessness that it appears to convey. Such a pessimistic and depressing outlook on life could, most certainly, be dangerous – but only if one were to blindly agree with the self-styled 'great' philosopher, and to fail to ask why a man with everything should be less happy than others who have nothing.

Many people today would sympathize with the view of life expressed by Ecclesiastes. Feelings of despair and detachment appear to be on the increase. Most people have become alienated from themselves (despite their obsessional concern for the self), from other people, from their environment, and from any sense of purpose. We appear to be drifting aimlessly in a self-created space of individual selves and perceived separateness.

Religious writer John Huddleston paints the picture of today's world as follows:

> In recent years it has become increasingly clear that the spiritual malaise described by writers and artists has deepened and spread rapidly. There are now too many manifestations at all levels of society and in a wide range of differing situations for the issue to be any longer ignored.
>
> Thus the majority of the poor in all countries feel they have no stake in society and that there is no hope for the future . . . there is a prevailing attitude of listlessness which periodically erupts into violent expressions of bitterness and frustration in which the poor themselves suffer the most.
>
> Those whom they envy and whom they see as their oppressors barely seem more satisfied. Many of the middle class find their only satisfaction in their job and the rest of their life is a desert. Even with regard to their occupation there is a growing disenchantment with the wearing, tearing, rat race. The boredom and frustration of private life produce reliance on sedatives and, in the case of the more prosperous, the psychiatrist's couch. The more adventurous try to escape from their frustrations in an ever-speeding round of frantic sex, descending to every conceivable permutation, or into frequent use of alcohol and drugs.
>
> The children of both rich and poor alike are increasingly disgusted by the empty materialism,

hypocrisy, and above all, loveless life of their elders, and feel completely alienated from established society.[16]

In addition to his reference to drugs and alcohol, Huddleston also points to the growing crime rate; a general decline in social morality, including petty dishonesty, deception, and the use of half-truths and lies in commercial advertising and politics; and a crumbling of respect for all forms of authority. These are all 'manifestations of an all-pervading spiritual sickness'.[17]

Writing on his view of the purpose of life, the philosopher Birch draws attention to a formlessness or yawning that exists in most people's lives. He identifies four different areas of struggle, or chaos, in our lives:

i)   Our inner chaos – an inability to live in harmony with oneself, to accept oneself, to discover one's identity, and to let body, feelings, and thought dwell together in friendship.

ii) Our social chaos – a lack of relatedness to others, an inability to live in harmony with others, and a failure to find common national and international goals.

iii) Our environmental chaos – pollution, and lack of rapport with our surroundings.

iv) Our metaphysical chaos – a sense of separation from the 'whole scheme of things', because we have no conviction that there is any scheme of things or values in the universe. Birch asks, 'If we have no value for the cosmos, can there be any value or meaning within human life, in human relationships, and in our relationship to our environment?'[18]

This lack of a sense of oneness with self, with others, with the world, and with the whole scheme of things has been given many names – such as disintegration, separation, alienation, disengagement, non-involvement, apathy, or estrangement. They all point to one thing – an illusion of separateness.

Our illusion of separateness leads only to feelings of emptiness and meaninglessness. The philosopher Ecclesiastes sums up our situation when he declares his life useless, despite his possessing everything in this world that most of us desire. His dilemma, however, and ours, arises from living life for the illusory self and failing to live life for the whole.

If a table could, somehow, identify itself as a flat piece of wood with four legs, but failed to attach any importance to the rest of the world around it, how could it establish any meaning for its existence? Meaning must always be taken from a broader context. If you ignore the broader context, you remove the meaning. The table might be able to declare, 'What a great table I am!' or 'What a beautiful table I am!', but as long as it fails to recognize the needs of the people who sit around it, what is its purpose? It is likely to proclaim, 'My existence is useless, all useless!'

This is a point that will be developed further in Part III, but the nub of the argument is this – if you create a separate self (whether or not it is extended to include family, possessions, and so on) and disregard anything which might exist beyond it (or value all outside it only as servants to the self), then the self must exist only to serve the self. That, I am arguing, leads to a state of meaninglessness.

SELF CONSCIOUSNESS

Where did the illusion of separateness come from? How did it develop? What, if anything, can we do about it? If the perceived separate self lies at the heart of our many contemporary social and psychological problems (as I have claimed in the previous chapter), then it is important to understand something of its origin and subsequent development. By tracing some of the major landmarks in the history of consciousness, I intend to provide the reader with a rough sketch of the path that we appear to be travelling along. A brief examination of the past may add to our understanding of the present and provide at least some basis for predicting the future (most of our predictions about the future are based on past observations). With a reasonably clear picture of where we are coming from, where we are now and where we are going to, we can begin to tackle the question of what we can do to change things. This question will be addressed later in Part III, but first, the origins and development of the separate self.

THE DEVELOPMENT OF SELF CONSCIOUSNESS

In the beginning there was Existence, One only, without a second . . . He, the One, thought to himself: Let me be many, let me grow forth. Thus out of himself he projected the universe; and having projected out of himself the universe, he entered into every being. All that is has itself in him alone. Of all things he is the subtle essence. He is the truth. He is the Self. And that . . . THAT ART THOU.

— *Chandogya Upanishad*[1]

The above version of events in the beginning was written approximately three thousand years ago in India. It is not very different from the standard model now accepted by modern scientists. In the standard or 'big bang' model of the universe, we also begin with an undifferentiated unity or 'singularity', which evolves into the multiplicity we now see.

Most scientists agree that our universe began around ten billion (10^{10}) years ago as a superdense fireball, which came into existence abruptly in a big bang. As the universe expanded into empty space, its density and temperature diminished, and the singularity began to take on different forms.

One second after the big bang, the temperature of the universe was about ten billion degrees, which is about a thousand times the temperature of the centre of our sun.[2] It was made up of a uniform mixture of subatomic particles, sometimes referred to by cosmologists as 'cosmic soup'.

Within the first few minutes, about twenty-five per cent of the nuclear material formed into the nuclei of the element helium, with a small amount of heavy hydrogen and other elements. The remaining seventy-five per cent was still unprocessed in the form of individual protons, which are the nuclei of hydrogen atoms.[3]

Most of the action, in the form of particle interactions, took place within the first four minutes.[4] During the next million years or so, the universe continued to cool and expand, without significant event, until the temperature dropped to a few thousand degrees. At this temperature, electrons and nuclei began to combine to form atoms. Matter took over from radiation as the dominant feature of the universe.[5]

The expansion was now less uniform, and began to slow down in some places as gravity came into play. Density in some parts of the universe was greater than in other parts, and some clumps of matter (in the form of hydrogen and helium gas) began to collapse under their own gravity. From these gravitational collapses, galaxies began to form.

Around one billion years after the initial big bang, stars began to form through the gravitational clustering of matter within the galaxies.[6] Out of the gases and heavier elements produced by the first generation stars, our own solar system was formed about five billion years ago. Our sun is a second or third generation star (which is now about halfway through its life expectancy).

The newly formed planets were initially very hot and without an atmosphere. As they cooled and developed atmospheres from gas emissions, complex molecular structures began to form. Conditions on earth (some time around four billion years ago) gave rise to the formation of primitive life forms, which contributed to the development and evolution of higher forms of life such as fish, reptiles and mammals.

Somewhere along the line, a simple consciousness arose. A further quantum leap in the evolutionary process took us from this level of simple (animal) consciousness to a completely new level of self (human) consciousness.[7] Homo sapiens, or 'man the wise', made an appearance about half a million years ago. To give some idea of just how recent this is, if the universe had come into existence one hundred years ago, then we would only have been born yesterday.

In the symbolism of the Bible story, Adam (the name in Hebrew means 'mankind') was not capable of forming concepts such as good or evil (and was, therefore, incapable of sin). The original Adam possessed only a simple consciousness. After eating the fruit of the tree of knowledge, he became aware of himself, he felt shame, and he acquired the sense of sin through knowledge of good and evil. He rose (or fell, according to the story) to a new level of consciousness – that of self consciousness. This was the beginning of the emergence of the separate self.

In possession of a new power which placed them at an advantage over the animals, our early ancestors were hunter-gatherers, and used stone tools for cutting, chopping, and hunting. The earliest farming communities did not begin to emerge until around 10,000 years ago. The advent of metal tools, about 5000 years later, was the next major milestone in human development.

This takes us to the era of Greco-Roman civilization, which brought with it a further rise in the level of consciousness and was the basis of western civilization today. From this point on, we began to philosophize about our existence. Out of this philosophy grew modern science, the latest step on the evolutionary ladder. This new mode of thinking was to play a major part in the creation of a fragmented view of the world, and would later contribute significantly to the development of the separate self.

The Milesians established the basis of physics in Greece around the sixth century BC (Thales of Miletus is generally regarded as the first true scientist). Up to that point, explanations had been based largely on myth. The Milesians relied a lot more on observation. Their philosophy, however, was still very much in keeping with ancient thought, with no distinction being drawn between animate and inanimate, or between mind and matter. This was a natural position for the ancients to adopt. Nature and humanity were not seen to be in opposition. This attitude to the surrounding world represents a fundamental difference between the ancients and ourselves. For us, the phenomenal world is primarily an 'it', whereas for primitive men and women, it was a 'thou'.[8] The intimate relationship that we once had with our world has been replaced with an exploitive one, and the sense of a separate self has subsequently become sharpened.

The new scientific mode of thinking was based on observation, which necessitated breaking the whole into parts and observing relationships between the parts. With the beginnings of classical scientific empiricism, the 'thou' of the ancients was on its way to becoming the 'it' that most of us now perceive around us. The observer was being separated from the observed, and the perception of oneness was developing into a perception of many.

The empirical methods of the Milesians in combination with Pythagoreanism helped to spawn a fragmented view of the world. A new breed of scientific mind–matter dualists emerged. The first of these, Anaxagoras (500–428 BC), regarded matter as being made up of 'seeds' and of mind said, 'Mind rules the world and has brought order out of confusion'.[9]

The most significant development for western science around this time was probably the introduction of 'basic building blocks' in a version of Atomism introduced by Democritus. Whilst the Atomism of Democritus did not break completely away from the earlier concept of oneness, it nevertheless admitted a plurality of beings (an infinite number of atoms). The idea of a division between spirit and matter was thus gaining ground, and during the fourth century BC, Aristotle systematized existing scientific knowledge and created a number of classifications, laws, and systems of formal logic that were to be the basis of the western view for almost 2000 years.

Aristotle was a pupil of Plato, but he digressed from his master's teachings by giving far more weight to observation than to the rationalist approach. Plato saw abstract forms or structures as the keys to understanding and describing the world, and appearance was, for him, of secondary importance. Aristotle founded deductive logic, by formulating syllogistic arguments, and promoted inductive procedures for science. On the subject of the One versus the many, he argued that it was necessary to advance from generalities to particulars (that is, from the whole to its parts), just as a child begins by calling all men 'father', and all women 'mother', but later on distinguishes each of them.[10]

Science continued to develop along the road of materialism and reductionism. Aristotle (although not a reductionist himself) made it clear that, for the new science of physics, the only fruitful way forward was through separation of the whole into its parts, which could then be analysed, classified, and ultimately comprehended. This approach was reinforced by later developments in geometry, mechanics, mathematics and astronomy (through the contributions of Euclid, Archimedes, Apollonius and Ptolemy, in particular).

It wasn't until the seventeenth century that the Copernican revolution (under the influence of Kepler and Galileo) overturned the old Ptolemaic system in astronomy, and the Newtonian revolution (based on foundations already laid by Galileo and Descartes) finally brought to an end the dominance of Aristotle's ideas in physics.

The success of these revolutionary systems helped to establish science as the dominant model for human thinking in the western world. Up until this point in our history, our view of the universe had been shaped largely by religious beliefs or superstition. The early work of Aristotle and Ptolemy was adopted by the Christian church as it fitted in well with their belief in a static Earth that had been created by God to occupy a central position in the universe.[11] We had been created in God's image and were His most exalted creatures, so it was only natural that everything (including the Sun) should revolve around us (this was the egocentric picture that had been propounded by both Aristotle and Ptolemy).

The Copernican model relegated our planet to a much less prominent position (as one of a number of planets revolving around the Sun) and received little support until it was promoted by Kepler and Galileo. The latter's support for the theory brought him into conflict with the Church, which considered itself the sole authority on all learning and investigation.[12] This was a battle that the Church ultimately lost. The way was opened for the search for answers outside the Church and religion.

Galileo helped science further along its way by laying the foundations of modern physics (which Newton was to build on later) through his experimental work and his laws of mechanics. He also introduced the division between objects and observers (an idea that was later reinforced by Descartes' distinction between mind and body), by dividing the properties of all physical objects into primary and secondary.[13] The primary properties, he regarded as those belonging 'objectively' to the object (properties that could be weighed or measured). Secondary properties were the 'subjective' ones arising from our sensations (perception of colour, taste, texture, and so on).

And so with the growing success of science, we began to look increasingly to reductionist explanations (which could be divorced from God) to help us to understand our world and our place in it. We began to distinguish between our selves (the 'subject') and the world around us ('objects'). Science could provide information about the relationships between the 'objects' around us, to enable us to predict and control events. Armed with Newton's Laws and our newly found scientific understanding, we could control our destiny by means other than prayer.

While scientists continued to develop their theories in relation to the material world of 'objects', philosophers turned their attention to matters of the mind (the 'subject' that perceived the 'objects'). If we could produce laws of mind in the same way as we had produced laws of motion, then we could extend our understanding to our selves (and possibly use it to control people in the same way that we had learned to control things). Our sense of self and our attempts to understand it grew, eventually, into a science of self. Out of the philosophy of mind and the methods of physics the science of psychology emerged in the nineteenth century.

THE SCIENCE OF SELF

Wilhelm Wundt founded the first formal laboratory of psychology at Leipzig in 1879. Around the same time, in the United States, William James began work on his now famous *Principles of Psychology*, which he finished in 1890. The new science continued to spread across Europe and America, and the beginning of the twentieth century saw the development of psychological tests for the measurement of intelligence by Binet in France, Cattell in the United States, and Spearman and Burt in England; the founding of psychoanalysis by Sigmund Freud in Austria; and the founding of behaviourism by John B. Watson in the United States. Up until the last twenty years or so, psychology was dominated by the perspectives of Freud and Watson, with most psychologists adhering to either the psychoanalytic or behaviourist paradigms.

Freud's radical ideas were first published in his *Interpretation of Dreams* in 1900, but they met with initial ridicule and another decade or more elapsed before his influence began to take hold. The name Freud and the term psychoanalysis were eventually to become synonymous with psychology.

Central to psychoanalysis is the tripartite division of the mind into the conscious, thinking *ego*; the childishly impulsive *id*, which operates at the level of sub-consciousness; and the *superego*, which acts as conscience and upholder of standards. As the drives of the id frequently run into conflict with the values and ideals imposed by the superego, a number of defence mechanisms are unconsciously employed to cope with this conflict. Psychologist Guy Claxton provides a clear and concise summary of these mechanisms as follows:

> In *repression* we forbid a conflict or one of its components to conscious awareness. In *projection* we attribute a disowned portion of ourselves to another person, scapegoating them for our own inadequacies. By *rationalizing* the mind spins itself a yarn that it can accept in mitigation ('Everybody does it', 'she kicked me first', etc. etc.). *Reaction formation* helps us to bury something of which we have been taught to be ashamed – sexuality and anger are the two most obvious candidates – by an exaggerated espousal of a contrary personality trait. By *regression* to a behaviour of a younger age a person can hope to persuade others (and himself) to lower their expectations about his degree of responsibility and maturity. *Displacement* enables us to direct our feelings – an angry outburst, let's say – not at the real object which may react in a threatening way (boss), but at another (spouse, children, cat) with whose reaction we can cope more easily. At a more pathological level *obsessions, compulsions* and *phobias* may be crippling, but may also have some avoidance value.[14]

The main drive that runs into trouble with the id is the sex drive. As this sexual energy is repressed by the unconscious processes of the superego, anxiety develops and this can often lead to neurosis or psychosis. Psychoanalysis seeks to uncover the source of conflict by analysing dreams, slips of the tongue, forgetfulness, and other clues from free-association that might indicate areas of repression. Once the source of anxiety is located, it can be brought out into the open and dealt with. That is a simplified synopsis of what is, in fact, an extremely complex theory.

Behaviourism developed from a paper by Watson, in 1913, entitled 'Psychology as the Behaviorist views it'.[15] This was essentially a reaction against the dominance, at that time, of the introspective approach that Wundt and his colleagues had fostered. Up until then, the characteristic method of formulating and testing hypotheses involved the introspection of one's own mind. Watson advocated 'objective' observation of behaviour, which could be viewed in terms of a response, or set of responses, to a particular stimulus, or set of stimuli. It was felt that such an approach would be more in line with that of other sciences, such as physics.

Out of behaviourism arose a whole new psychology of learning (modern approaches to animal learning are still based on behaviourist techniques), and a new approach to treatment in the form of behaviour therapy. At the core of this approach lies the attempt to change or shape behaviour by means of reward and/or punishment.

Like psychoanalysis, behaviourism developed into a highly complex system with a variety of schools of thought. The dominance of both perspectives in psychology lasted for over half a century. Then, during the fifties and sixties, a number of undercurrents began to erode that position. One of these undercurrents was the new 'third force' of humanistic psychology.

Behaviourism, in its quest for objectivity, excluded the subjective data of consciousness, while psychoanalysis reduced behaviour to an expression of unconscious drives. Human phenomena such as love, personal freedom, art, literature and religion were largely neglected, or explained away in terms of stimulus–response chains or manifestations of unconscious forces, by what was increasingly becoming a dehumanizing science. Humanistic psychology arose in reaction to the mechanistic and deterministic views of humanity that were espoused by behaviourists and psychoanalysts.

More than any other area of psychology, the new humanistic psychology focused on the self. Its initial concern for humanity very quickly developed into a concern for self-fulfilment. The science of self, rooted in the study of the workings of the mind and its behavioural manifestations, began to blossom in the study of human (self) potential.

In 1957 and 1958, Abraham Maslow and Clark Moustakas invited psychologists to attend two meetings in Detroit with the aim of founding a professional association dedicated to a more meaningful, more humanistic vision. They discussed a number of themes that they felt were being neglected by mainstream psychology at that time. The success of these meetings led to the establishment of the *Journal of Humanistic Psychology* in 1961, and to the founding of the Association for Humanistic Psychology later in the same year.[16]

A former president of the Association, Floyd Matson, sums up the situation as follows:

What we were against was man's inhumanity to man, everywhere in the world but specifically in the laboratories and consulting rooms of our profession. And what we were for was the humanity of man in those same places. In the labs of the humanists, analysis gave up its priority to synthesis; in their clinics, diagnosis gave way to dialogue. To be humanistic meant among other things, to be holistic: to see man as a whole; not as a pure reason, nor as mere mechanism, but as a unity of heart, mind, and even spleen.[17]

The 'third force' of humanistic psychology has grown considerably in recent years.[18] The Association for Humanistic Psychology is now a worldwide organization, which continues to exert a growing influence on mainstream psychology. The following statement, made recently by the Association, gives some idea of its scope:

Humanistic psychologists today are a diverse group of people on every continent. They include therapists, theorists, educators, managers, healthcare professionals and people from other occupations who embrace a commitment to human development. Although most of the psychologists identify with schools commonly thought of as part of the Third Force – existential, gestalt, Eastern traditions, Rogerian, transpersonal, etc. – there are also many behavioral therapists, Jungians, neo-Freudians and others representing modern variations on the old First and Second Forces. On the whole these distinctions are now far less important than the overriding commitment to understanding the full, paradoxical and profoundly complex human condition, a commitment that extends to many humanistic persons who are not psychologists, but who accept and live this humanistic vision personally, professionally and societally.[19]

In its commitment to the development of human potential, humanistic psychology recognizes the need to combine individual freedom with interdependence and responsibility to one another as members of groups and organizations and of society as a whole. It acknowledges that we can never be completely free from societal and unconscious forces, but nevertheless emphasizes the independent dignity and worth of human beings and their capacity to develop personal competence and self-respect. Given the free will that individuals have, they are expected to use it to fulfil their potential, or to achieve 'self-actualization'.

Abraham Maslow outlined the characteristics of this 'self-actualization' as follows:[20]

1) Superior perception of reality.
2) Increased acceptance of self, others and nature.
3) Increased spontaneity and greatly increased creativity.
4) Increased autonomy and resistance to enculturation.
5) Richness of emotional reaction.
6) Increased identification with the human species.
7) Changed interpersonal relationships.
8) Change in values and a more democratic value structure.
9) An ability for mystical/spiritual experiences (or 'peak' experiences).

Another leading figure in the humanistic movement, Carl Rogers, also embraced the concept of 'self-actualization'. Rogers' 'Self Theory' focuses on individuals' self-concept, their personal experience and their subjective interpretation of environmental stimuli.[21] Of particular importance is any perceived threat to the self-concept. Consequently, his therapy involved giving the individual the opportunity to reorganize his or her subjective world, and to thereby integrate and 'actualize' the self. His aim was to help the individual to become a more autonomous, spontaneous and confident person.

In addition to this focus on human growth through personal growth, humanistic psychologists, working through the Association for Humanistic Psychology, are also involved in 'humanistic activism', which seeks 'to introduce humanistic principles into public policy decision-making and to have a positive impact upon world peace, social justice, planetary survival and other important issues that confront humanity'.[22]

The humanistic perspective embraces the individual's subjective position within a holistic framework. It takes account of the uniqueness of the individual, the individual's perception of the situation, and all factors pertaining to that situation. It avoids an oversimplification of reality, yet, at the same time, it provides a great deal of insight into human thought and behaviour.

Humanistic psychology covers a wide range of phenomena normally by-passed by the more traditional approaches – phenomena such as personal meanings, 'common sense', imagination, fantasy, religious belief, mystical and unusual experiences, altered states of consciousness, and various eastern philosophies.[23] Its application includes personal growth, counselling, psychotherapy, education, organizational development, social action and community development.[24]

A number of recent developments in therapeutic techniques have arisen from the humanistic school. These include the Gestalt therapy of Frederick Perls, various counselling techniques, encounter groups, body awareness, role-play, meditation, and the use of drama.[25] Various 'new paradigm' research methods have also been linked to the movement.[26] These include attempts to combine subjectivity with objectivity (for example, subjective reports of participants used to complement observations of researchers), and the involvement of research subjects as 'co-researchers'.

Although, as British psychologist Helen Graham points out,[27] humanistic psychology is still far from being a complete unified theory, and may better be described as a loose connection of models, ideas and therapeutic techniques, its adherents share the conviction that we have the potential to be much more than we are at present, both as individuals and as a community. In the words of the mystic, Johannes Tauler, 'If I were a king and did not know it, I would not be a king'.[28]

The goals of humanistic psychology are laudable. However, the practice and limited vision of some of its adherents, unfortunately, falls far short of Abraham Maslow's original vision. In fact, Maslow saw the new 'third force' psychology as merely a transient stage in the development of a much broader 'fourth force' psychology that would take us beyond the self. In the meantime, the self appears to be receiving more attention than the community, and individual growth plays a greater part in mainstream psychology than does universal growth. So much so that some writers have now branded psychology 'the cult of self-worship'. Christian writer Dave Hunt summarizes this point of view as follows:

> Salvation always centers on *Self*: self-confidence, self-potential, self-awareness, self-acceptance, self-love, self-image, self-esteem, self-fulfilment, self-development, self-assertion, self-actualization, self-ad nauseam![29]

Hunt argues that Abraham Maslow was responsible for crowning psychology's deification of the self by declaring self-actualization to be the highest human goal. He claims that the current movement towards eastern mysticism (as is taking place in some areas of the new psychology) is a dangerous return to occultism. The danger, he claims, arises from its denial of moral absolutes and its deification of the self. James Sire is another writer who expresses concern about the threat to morality.

> If the self is king, why worry about ethics? The king can do no wrong. If the self is satisfied, that is sufficient. Such a conception allows for the grossest cruelty. In other words, the new consciousness world view falls prey to all the pitfalls of solipsism and egoism.[30]

Within psychology itself it has also been claimed that the most serious charge against humanistic psychology is its promotion of a narcissistic, selfish and hedonistic trend.[31] This is certainly apparent from the humanistic focus on self-development generally, and in the Gestalt Prayer of Frederick Perls in particular.

> I do my thing, and you do your thing.
> I am not in this world to live up to your expectations,
> And you are not in this world to live up to mine.
> You are you, and I am I,
> And if by chance we find each other, it's beautiful.
> If not, it can't be helped.[32]

Science writer Martin Gardner is also very critical of the extremist element of pseudoscientists, cranks and charlatans that have either been spawned by or attracted to the growth circuit of the new psychology. An example of his attitude to the new consciousness movement, which has developed out of humanistic psychology, is his highly critical, but humorous, review of Adam Smith's *Powers of Mind* – a book aimed at 'middle-classers eager to find instant health and happiness'.

Of course it's not called happiness. You raise your consciousness, expand your inner space, increase your aliveness. To give fake credibility to his short-cut tour of what he calls the 'consciousness circuit', Smith practices the old technique of first making a tour himself . . . Doctors give Smith little lectures on placebos, on drugs, on the Rumpelstiltskin effect (naming an ailment makes a patient get better), on split-brain research. After instruction by an *I Ching* master, Smith asks the book's advice on stock investments. He visits Esalen. He studies Arica. His body is pummeled in a Rolfing session . . . He takes a biofeedback course. He tries Yoga. He does the sliced-ping-pong-balls-over-the-eyes bit with Montague Ullman at the Maimonides Dream Lab. He floats in John Lilly's sensory deprivation tank. He half practices TM and discloses (shame!) his secret mantra . . . Several chapters cover Zen sports: Zen football, Zen golf, Zen tennis (no Zen bowling?). The Guru Maharaj Ji and the Reverend Sun Moon are passed over lightly because Smith failed to contact them, but he did meet Uri Geller, and he *thinks* he met the elusive Carlos Castaneda . . . Baba Ram Dass gets a big play. Ram Dass is Richard Alpert, Tim Leary's old sidekick at Harvard before the two were sidekicked off the Yard. Alpert went to India, came back a guru. He is now much admired on the college consciousness circuit, even though his father (president of the New Haven Railroad) calls him Rum Dum and his older brother calls him Rammed Ass.[33]

Needless to say, Gardner is not impressed by any of the 'new strawberry short cuts' to happiness or 'raised consciousness'. This comes across clearly in his treatment of EST (a technique that purports to help people attain enlightenment) in the same review.

EST is Latin for 'is.' What is, is. What isn't, isn't. The universe is what it is. It can't be anything else. It's perfect. You are one of its machines. You are what you are. You, too, are perfect. You have 'free will' but in a paradoxical sense. You have to choose what you choose. The secret of satori is to relax and enjoy. 'The whole idea of making it,' Erhard told Smith, 'is bullshit.' In fact, everything is bullshit, including EST. Once you recognize this great truth, and that there is nothing to get, you 'get it.' You lose, of course, your $250 initiation fee. That's what EST gets.[34]

The problem lies in distinguishing the wheat from the chaff, and there appears to be a lot of chaff about. Quite a few cranks and charlatans have jumped on to the human potential bandwagon. These people make scientific claims, arising from (in Gardner's terms) delusions of scientific competence or a desire to make some money from an eager and gullible bunch of 'shortcutters'. Guy Claxton sums up the situation very well.

Growth has become the growth industry, and therapies and groups are advertised with the same enthusiasm and disregard for the facts as snake oil. Heaven is just a weekend away, and This Book Will Change Your Life . . . the creation of false expectations can and does lead people to follow the growth circuit, from one high-cum-disappointment to the next, in search of the one that really works. And there is plenty to choose from: encounter, bioenergetics, massage, postural integration, enlightenment intensives, rolfing, *est*, primal scream, rebirthing (three kinds), transactional analysis, sufi dancing, tai chi, Alexander, reflexology, shiatsu, transcendental meditation, zazen, regression, Reichian bodywork, psychosynthesis, gestalt groups, marathons, synanon, . . . the list is endless. Carried away by promises of increased self-confidence, better orgasms and more satisfying relationships, it is hard not to pick up the idea that the good life is eternally happy and problem-free. This attitude generates good business for the industry, because it makes the punter even more dissatisfied with his own confused little life, and ensures his constant return.[35]

The human potential movement at Esalen, which grew out of the new humanistic psychology, also attracted a number of people whose interests lay somewhere outside the realms of science. The publicity surrounding nude bathing, nude encountering, and the use of techniques such as 'touch therapy' at Esalen, led to it being viewed as a hedonist's paradise. Frederick Perls, one of the movement's most influential figures, left Esalen after becoming disenchanted with 'turner-onners' and 'quacks and con-men', with their emphasis on 'instant cure, instant joy, instant sensory awareness, and instant enlightenment'.[36]

Although few psychologists actually advocate living life only for the self, much of what is said by psychologists could be construed in that way. Add to this the crankish element, who appear to gain more attention than the serious scientists, and you get a distorted picture of psychology as the 'cult of self-worship'. Unfortunately, this element currently influences the lives of a large number of people in our society. The message of modern psychology has been truncated to read 'know yourself and improve yourself'. The bit concerning the oneness of humanity has been conveniently omitted by the self-serving promoters of self-fulfilment.

THE SELF AS GOD

As the sense of a separate self continued to grow, the sense of God began to decline. With materialistic science came secularization. The answers provided by the Church to many of life's questions were not in accord with those provided by science, which was, after all, proving itself more successful than the Church in improving our material conditions and comfort. The hypocrisy of many of the Church's priests and bishops was no longer acceptable in comparison with a fair-minded and dogma-free science.

The sixteenth and seventeenth centuries had witnessed terrible religious wars in Europe.[37] By the end of the seventeenth century, people were impressed by the Scientific Revolution and at the same time tired of religious strife. It is not, therefore, surprising that with the eighteenth century came the 'Age of Reason' and the so-called Enlightenment – the advent of modern scepticism and the decline of religious beliefs. By the nineteenth century, Friedrich Nietzsche was announcing the death of God, and Karl Marx was declaring religion to be 'the opium of the masses'.

The publication of Darwin's *The Origin of Species*, in 1859, and of Lyell's *The Geological Evidence of the Antiquity of Man*, in 1863, demonstrated that the earth was much older than the 6000 years attributed to it by the Church, and that there was something wrong with the literal interpretation that had been applied to the story of creation in the Bible.[38] Just as they had opposed Galileo, earlier, for threatening their earth-centred view of the universe, the Church entered into yet another confrontation with science on the theory of evolution. This was to be another lost battle that would contribute to the decline of the Church as a point of absolute authority.

The work of the depth psychologists (those concerned with the unconscious), particularly that of Freud, at the beginning of the twentieth century, was to further undermine the religious edifice. Problems of the mind had previously been designated spiritual, and were consequently dealt with, to some extent, by priests and ministers. Treatment by counselling or through communion with God was deemed appropriate – more severe cases of mental illness would have been treated by inflicting some form of physical unpleasantness or pain, which included boring holes in the head to release the evil spirits.[39] This particular role of the Church was now taken over by the psychoanalyst. The religious urge, for Freud, was merely an illusory rationalization of unconscious wishes – a projection of a father-image, in the form of God, to compensate for our infantile sense of helplessness.[40]

The contribution of science and humanism to the decline of the Christian Church is neatly summarized by the religious writer, F.C. Happold:

> Modern man, it is said, has opted for a secular world; he has come of age; he has no longer any need of religion . . . It has been, not the Christian Church, but the scientists and humanists who have led the advance in the march towards toleration and free inquiry and towards social justice and a better life for the common man. In spite of its saints, mystics, and martyrs, the history of the Christian Church is a sorry one. It is far too much the story of intolerance, persecution and bigotry, of inquisitions, torture and burnings, of 'images' of God which had little resemblance to the loving Father or our Lord Jesus Christ, or to the inner Christ of St Paul.[41]

John Huddleston, in a brief résumé of the rise and fall of the Christian Church, points to its very success being instrumental in its downfall:

In the glorious days of its early history the Christian Church, besides being a centre of learning, was also undoubtedly responsible for the raising of standards of civilization at all levels of society. Unfortunately its very success became the source of its undoing. The Church became a power in its own right, it became involved in politics and closely thereafter corruption followed. Such activities as the Crusades, the sale of indulgences, the Inquisition, to say nothing of the low personal moral standards of many churchmen, caused doubt as to the Church's loyalty to the teachings of Jesus, and its claim to be the spiritual guide for mankind . . . . The bishops built beautiful churches and lived in luxury, and sent their priests out to tell the poor to accept their lot . . . Laws on birth-control, inter-faith marriages, divorce, medical care, burials, and other personal matters have been harshly enforced without regard to the circumstances of peoples' lives or to the ultimate purpose of religion. In consequence, instead of becoming a means for raising up the human spirit, religious laws have frequently become instruments of oppression.[42]

The result of all this is what we now refer to as secularization, a turning away from religion, and a state of mind which, Huddleston feels, is reflected in the attitudes of the churchgoing public today:

The hypocrisy of churchgoing has become a byword. Many of those who go to church do so without enthusiasm, only to preserve a respectable social image, or at best as a gesture of conscience to be indulged in on Sunday, but to be forgotten for the rest of the week.[43]

The problem of secularization is not confined to the Christian Church. Harold Kushner identifies the same 'spiritual vacuum' amongst modern Jews, who appear to have a similar attitude to synagogue attendance as Christians have to church attendance.[44]

The religious world-view has, to a large extent, been replaced by a scientific world-view. As physicist Anjam Khursheed puts it, 'the past four hundred years have taught us to think of science and religion as pitifully unequal contestants in a struggle for our hearts and minds', and 'the scientists seem to have won'.[45] Most of us feel that the Church has no longer anything to offer in terms of either explanation or guidance (although it may still offer something socially). If we want something explained, we can turn to scientific theory. If we want guidance, we can turn to a psychologist or a counsellor (who will, in turn, apply scientific theory).

So what happens when you remove God from the equation? Nothing much, you might argue. We no longer need Him as a means of explanation – physicists now believe that they are on the verge of explaining everything (just as they believed towards the end of the last century!). We no longer need a father figure; we have come of age. Just like adolescents (which is arguably the level of consciousness that the species has now attained), we know what is best for us without looking beyond ourselves for help. Under the influence of the new science of self, we have identified the ultimate goal – the goal of self-fulfilment. We no longer need to live our lives for God (who or what is He anyway?). We can live our lives for the self (at least we know it exists – we have self consciousness!). We can even extend our sense of self to include family, possessions, team, social group, nation, and so on as and when it suits us. So, who needs God?

Perhaps we should think again. We should consider the feelings of meaninglessness and emptiness, of alienation and even depression that many of us now experience. These mental states are linked to so many of the problems of modern society, from substance abuse and family conflict to violence and crime. As Alfred Adler, founder of Individual Psychology notes, 'It is the individual who is not interested in his fellow human beings who has the greatest difficulties in life, and causes the greatest injury to others.'[46] Science has brought us many material gains, but it has also brought with it a spiritual loss.

To celebrate its fiftieth birthday, the government's Central Statistical Office recently published a little card showing how the United Kingdom has changed during its lifetime.[47] Compared with our predecessors (probably our grandparents) of fifty years ago, we now have about two and a half times their purchasing power (we can buy two and a half times as much with our earnings); we work shorter hours; we are about ten times as likely to own a car; we are about twice as likely to own our own home; our young people are six times as likely to receive a university education; and we can expect to live twenty per cent longer. We are also about three times as likely to go on strike; about ten times as likely to become victims of a crime; and over twenty times as likely to get divorced. Dare I suggest an inverse relationship between material gain and psychological health?

Interestingly, it was just over fifty years ago that Carl Jung wrote about the social and psychological malaise that had resulted from our exclusion of God:

Modern man does not understand how much his 'rationalism' . . . has put him at the mercy of the psychic 'underworld'. He has freed himself from 'super-stition' (or so he believes), but in the process he has lost his spiritual values to a positively dangerous degree. His moral and spiritual tradition has disintegrated, and he is now paying the price for this break-up in worldwide disorganization and dissociation.

Anthropologists have often described what happens to a primitive society when its spiritual values are exposed to the impact of modern civilization. Its people lose the meaning of their lives, their social organization disintegrates, and they themselves morally decay. We are now in the same condition.[48]

Have we replaced God with the self? Have we, like Nietzsche, declared God to be dead? Nietzsche, in the end, drifted into a state of mental illness from which he never recovered. Can we afford to continue any further down that same road?

PART TWO

....

THE
PHYSICAL
UNIVERSE

PERCEPTIONS
OF
REALITY

> Whether the universe is a concourse of atoms, or
> nature is a system, let this first be established, that I
> am a part of the whole which is governed by nature;
> next, I am intimately related to the parts which are of
> the same kind with myself.
>
> — *Marcus Aurelius*[1]

Chapter One described four major problems arising from
our fragmented view of the universe – the futile search
for absolute causes or reasons; the search for a self that
continues to elude us; our indifference to the rest of the
world that we perceive to be separated from us; and our
feelings of alienation and meaninglessness. Self consciousness and the illusion of separateness are seen to be the
underlying roots of these problems.

Chapter Two attempted to trace the development of
these twin manifestations. They are interrelated aspects of
human consciousness arising from the evolutionary process,
which took us from simple consciousness to a more complex
level of thought involving categorization. Instead of flowing

with nature, as the simple creatures we once were must have done, we now find ourselves defining everything in terms of 'it' and 'not it'. This latest development may be viewed as the 'self consciousness' stage in human evolution, as it enables us to distinguish between 'self' and 'not self'. The sense of separateness and the sense of self, however, appear to have been sharpened over the past three centuries or so through the growing influence of scientific models of reality and the decline of religious beliefs. Where religion helped to hold the perceived pieces of our world together (initially through a limited number of gods, and more recently through a single, omnipresent, omnipotent, omniscient God), science has in the past led to a further breaking of the pieces in its search for answers.

This chapter will examine more closely our scientific view of the universe, noting particularly the recent movement towards holism and the search for unity. This will preface an attempt (in Chapter Four) to produce a unified theory by bringing various strands of physics and psychology together.

MODELS OF REALITY

> Through space the universe grasps me and swallows me up like a speck; through thought I grasp it.
> — *Pascal*[2]

Each of us 'grasps' the universe in our own way. We comprehend our world by breaking it down into parts, and by building it up again in a variety of models that contain a selection of parts and hypothesized relationships between them. Too often, we fail to recognize the limitations of our models. We forget that we are merely applying models to the world and are not in possession of some absolute truth. We even find it surprising that the rest of the world should fail to subscribe to our discovered, or adopted, truth. We chide others for being too stupid or misguided to see things as they 'really' are.

No single person has access to the whole of reality. We each hold in our heads some form of conceptual framework for a reality 'out there', which encompasses us in some way. Each of these versions of reality will reflect our sense of self (more of this in the next chapter). Our picture of the universe must contain a self and non-self that relate to each other. If the self and non-self (which we believe to be there to serve the self) are not compatible, then the picture will quickly disintegrate. This means that there are about five billion (5,000,000,000) individual realities in our world at present. At lower levels of consciousness, there are many more animal, vegetable and mineral realities that exist on our planet. Beyond that again, there is a whole universe of reality, about which we know little or next to nothing. The reality we perceive and experience, then, is but an infinitesimal and unique subset of the whole of reality.

In attempting to grasp the whole of reality, we employ a variety of scientific theories, philosophies and religious world views. These frameworks help us to interpret and order the world around us. They also change over time, under a variety of social and political influences.

It is difficult to see how we could make sense of the world without using models, but a major drawback arises from their self-fulfilling or self-validating nature. What we see is largely a function of what we expect to see. In fitting the data of experience to our existing models, we provide further 'evidence' in support of them. Thus, according to psychologists Walsh and Vaughan, 'the Freudian analyst looking for sexual libido as the prime motivator, the Adlerian analyst searching for superiority strivings, and the behaviorist examining for environmental reinforcers, are all likely to be successful in their search'.[3]

Because we are using our models to 'see' the world, it is difficult for us to see more than they allow us to see. As Walsh and Vaughan argue, they are 'self-fulfilling, self-prophetic organizers of experience that modify perception'. This point was vividly illustrated, over one hundred years ago, by Edwin Abbott in his remarkable story of *Flatland*. The story is narrated by one of the inhabitants of Flatland – a Square. He begins by describing his two-dimensional world to the 'happy readers, who are privileged to live in space'.

> Imagine a vast sheet of paper on which straight Lines, Triangles, Squares, Pentagons, Hexagons, and other figures, instead of remaining fixed in their places, move freely about, on or in the surface, but without the power of rising above or sinking below it, very much like shadows – only hard and with luminous edges – and you will then have a pretty correct notion of my country and countrymen.[4]

In a disturbing dream, the Square visits the one-dimensional world of Lineland. He attempts to describe himself to the Linelanders as a Line of Lines, coming from a world where you can move not only from point to point, but also from side to side. He is about to be attacked by the angry Linelanders when he awakens.

The Square later has an encounter with an inhabitant of Spaceland – a peculiar Circle who seems to change in size, and even disappear. The visitor explains that he is a Sphere from a three-dimensional world, and describes himself as a Circle of Circles. He informs the Square that his size only appears to change as he moves towards him or away from him in a third dimension of Space. Realizing, however, that argument alone will not convince the Square, the Sphere creates an experience of depth for him.

After gaining this insight into another dimension, the Square becomes an evangelist and attempts to convince his fellow Flatlanders of the existence of Space. He is so insistent that the Chief Circle finally orders his imprisonment, for 'the public good'.

In another little story with a big message, Jean-Paul Sartre's *No Exit* tells of some people trapped in a self-imposed 'hell' – one room, no windows, crowded together and unable to leave. After a long time in 'hell', a door was opened and they were free to leave. However, they chose to stay because they feared the unknown. They had become comfortable with their life in 'hell'.[5]

Just as the people in Sartre's story became comfortable with their self-imposed limited existence, so we become comfortable with our limited models, despite their obvious incompleteness. In the same way, the Flatlanders were comfortable with their two-dimensional view of the world, and felt threatened when the Square attempted to thrust an alien view upon them.

We should, therefore, be wary of complacent acceptance of our own limited models as some form of absolute truth. For unless your point of view is all-encompassing (and you are in the fortunate position of sharing the Mind of God), then your truth must be relative.

We should remember that our views, theories, ideas, beliefs, models of reality, or whatever we want to call them, are not only incomplete, but also relative to our unique experience of life. We should also remember that our models of reality *are* just models. We extract from reality various discernible patterns or recurring themes, which we associate with each other to form models that give our world meaning. We can continuously update our models to improve their fit with the data of experience, or we can limit our experience and attend only to data that fits our models.

The limitation of our models is highlighted by the economist E.F. Schumacher in his analysis of 'the four great Levels of Being' – mineral, plant, animal and human. These four Levels of Being are likened to an inverted pyramid where each higher level comprises everything lower and is open to influences from everything higher. None of the lower levels are 'adequate' to the task of comprehending the higher levels. Just as a plant cannot be expected to comprehend life at the animal level, animals (so far as we know) cannot comprehend life at the human level, and we are inadequate to the task of comprehending any level of being above our own.[6]

Within the human level of being, each of us has our own personal level of being. The 'higher' the level, the greater and richer the experience, and the greater the level of understanding. At a low level of being, only an impoverished kind of existence is possible. A person entirely fixed in the philosophy of materialistic scientism, confining attention only to what can be measured, counted, or weighed, will therefore experience the world as a meaningless wasteland. Similarly, people who limit themselves to biological needs and creature comforts will inevitably live a miserable life. If the world is seen as nothing more than a chaos of particles without purpose or meaning, then we will *understand* everything, including humanity, from that perspective, and reduce our experience to that of a participant in a mere cosmic accident of no consequence whatsoever.

The main point is this – 'Nothing can be known without there being an appropriate "instrument" in the make-up of the knower . . . the understanding of the knower must be *adequate* to the thing to be known'.[7] G.N.M. Tyrell in his book *Grades of Significance* puts it this way:

Take a book, for example. To an animal a book is merely a coloured shape. Any higher significance a book may hold lies above the level of its thought. And the book *is* a coloured shape; the animal is not wrong. To go a step higher, an uneducated savage may regard a book as a series of marks on paper. This is the book seen on a higher level of significance than the animal's, the one which corresponds to the savage's level of thought. Again it is not wrong, only the book *can* mean more. It may mean a series of letters arranged according to certain rules. This is the book on a higher level of significance than the savage's . . . Or finally, on a still higher level, the book may be an expression of meaning.[8]

In other words, what we 'see' is determined in part by the level of knowledge that we bring with us to the situation, and since acquired knowledge varies considerably from person to person (depending on social and cultural background, experience, interests, and so on) there are inevitably many things which some people 'see' while others cannot. Our perceptions and theories are shaped by our unique beliefs and the unique set of social experiences we have encountered in the past. Our models of reality are dynamic cognitive structures, which are constantly shaped by a combination of social, psychological, biological and environmental influences. Schumacher sums up the importance of social influence in the following statement:

In short, when dealing with something representing a higher grade of significance or Level of Being than inanimate matter, the observer depends not only on the adequateness of his own higher qualities, perhaps 'developed' through learning and training; he also depends on the adequateness of his 'faith' or, to put it more conventionally, of his fundamental presuppositions and basic assumptions. In this respect he tends to be very much a child of his time and of the civilisation in which he has spent his formative years; for the human mind, generally speaking, does not just think: it thinks with ideas, most of which it simply adopts and takes over from surrounding society.[9]

Like the inhabitants of Flatland, our understanding of the world will, therefore, be determined by our 'adequateness' to the task of understanding. Through our models we glimpse only a part of the total picture. We must accept that differing and apparently conflicting views of the world can all be true at the same time. Although it is not always immediately clear that reconciliation of different views is possible, it may sometimes be achieved by moving to a higher level of analysis. A combination of theories will usually account better for something than a single theory. This, of course, is what the famous physicist Niels Bohr insisted upon when he first proposed his principle of Complementarity in 1927.[10]

Here is a beautiful and relevant piece of dialogue by Jauch, which is quoted by Douglas Hofstadter in his book *Godel, Escher, Bach: An Eternal Golden Braid*[11]:

SALVIATI Suppose I give you two sequences of numbers, such as 7 8 5 3 9 8 1 6 3 3 9 7 4 4 8 3 0 9 6 1 5 6 6 0 8 4 ... and 1, –1/3, +1/5, –1/7, +1/9, –1/11, +1/13, –1/15, ...
If I asked you, Simplicio, what the next number of the first sequence is, what would you say?
SIMPLICIO I could not tell you. I think it is a random sequence and that there is no law to it.
SALVIATI And for the second sequence?
SIMPLICIO That would be easy. It must be +1/17.

SALVIATI Right. But what would you say if I told you that the first sequence is also constructed by a law and this law is in fact identical with the one you have just discovered for the second sequence?

SIMPLICIO This does not seem probable to me.

SALVIATI But it is indeed so, since the first sequence is simply the beginning of the decimal fraction [expansion] of the sum of the second. Its value is $\pi/4$.

SIMPLICIO You are full of such mathematical tricks, but I do not see what this has to do with abstraction and reality.

SALVIATI The relationship with abstraction is easy to see. The first sequence looks random unless one has developed through a process of abstraction a kind of filter which sees a simple structure behind the apparent randomness.

It is exactly in this manner that laws of nature are discovered. Nature presents us with a host of phenomena which appear mostly as chaotic randomness until we select some significant events and abstract from their particular, irrelevant circumstances so that they become idealized. Only then can they exhibit their true structure in full splendor.

SAGREDO This is a marvelous idea! It suggests that when we try to understand nature, we should look at the phenomena as if they were *messages* to be understood. Except that each message appears to be random until we establish a code to read it. This code takes the form of an abstraction, that is, we choose to ignore certain things as irrelevant and we thus partially select the content of the message by a free choice. These irrelevant signals form the 'background noise', which will limit the accuracy of our message.

But since the code is not absolute there may be several messages in the same raw material of the data, so changing the code will result in a message of equally deep significance in something that was merely noise before, and *conversely*: In a new code a former message may be devoid of meaning.

Thus a code presupposes a free choice among different, complementary aspects, each of which has equal claim to *reality*, if I may use this dubious word.

Some of these aspects may be completely unknown to us now but they may reveal themselves to an observer with a different system of abstractions.

But tell me, Salviati, how can we then claim that we *discover* something out there in the objective real world? Does this not mean that we are merely creating things according to our own images and that reality is only within ourselves?

SALVIATI I don't think that this is necessarily so, but it is a question which requires deeper reflection.

It is certainly a question that I shall be reflecting on later, but first let us consider the abstractions of science on the nature of reality.

THE PHYSICIST'S WORLD

Whilst most of us don't stop to ask too many questions about the physical composition and dynamics of our world, we are nonetheless influenced by the models created by scientists. The classical scientific view of the world as a machine, containing an unimaginable number of parts that interact according to certain physical laws, has influenced our thinking and attitudes since the time of Aristotle. This view has undoubtedly contributed to our sense of an independent self that can, with the aid of science, manipulate and exploit a machine-like world for our own ends. A new scientific view is now emerging to change this attitude. Although the classical models reinforced and most likely contributed to what I have referred to earlier as the 'illusion of separateness', the new physics suggests the possibility of bringing the self and the world back together again.

i) Newton's World

In 1687, Isaac Newton published one of the most important single works in the history of modern science, the *Philosophiae Naturalis Principia Mathematica (Mathematical Principles of Natural Philosophy)*. At the centre of this revolutionary work lay his three laws of motion (based on the earlier work of Galileo):

1) if a body is at rest or moving at a constant speed in a straight line, it will remain in that same condition until acted upon by a force;

2) the rate of change of the velocity, or acceleration, is directly proportional to the force and inversely proportional to the mass of the body;

3) the actions of two bodies upon each other are always equal and directly opposite (that is, reaction is always equal and opposite to action);

and his law of gravitation:

4) any particle of matter in the universe attracts any other with a force directly proportional to the product of their masses and inversely proportional to the square of the distance between them.

These laws formed the basis of a scientific reality that took over from the old ideas of Aristotle (which included notions such as: light bodies rise naturally away from the centre of the earth, while heavy bodies move toward it with a speed relative to their weight).

To this day, calculations for modern space flight still employ Newton's laws, and the vast majority of people (unknowingly) base their perceptions of reality on his view of the world – a fragmented and mechanistic view of separate bodies moving around in reaction to invisible forces within a three-dimensional space, with change constantly taking place over something called time.

By the end of the nineteenth century, there seemed to be very little that could not be explained in terms of the Newtonian mechanical model. Physicists saw the material world as being composed of very small hard objects, called atoms, that interacted with one another to produce the variety of materials, living and non-living, that we see around us. Light was something that was propagated in the form of electromagnetic waves (Maxwell had earlier demonstrated that light, magneticism and electricity were one and the same phenomenon). The division of the world into particles and waves seemed clear-cut, and 'physics seemed to be on the threshold of dotting all the i's and crossing the t's'.[12] A number of developments at the beginning of the twentieth century, however, soon shattered this optimism.

ii) The Quantum World

One of the i's that classical physicists still had to dot was the problem of black body radiation. When you raise the temperature of a black piece of iron, for example, by placing it in a fire, it turns red, and eventually white if left long enough. According to calculations using Newton's laws, it should glow bright blue at all temperatures.[13]

In 1900, Max Planck resolved the problem. He proposed that energy (light, heat, or any other form of electromagnetic radiation) must be absorbed and emitted in discrete packets, and not in a continuous manner as was previously believed (which explains why black bodies do not absorb and emit infinite amounts of energy). He called these packets of energy *quanta*. This was the beginning of quantum theory. Its general acceptance into mainstream physics, however, was far from immediate (Planck did not receive official recognition for his work until 1918, when he received the Nobel Prize).

In 1905, Einstein made a further contribution to the new quantum theory by introducing the *photon* (a particle of light). In proposing that light sometimes acted as a stream of particles, called photons, Einstein made no attempt to refute the already established wave-like nature of light. However, it was still difficult for most physicists of the time to accept that something could be both a wave and a particle, and it was 1921 before Einstein received his Nobel Prize for this contribution (surprisingly, he did not receive similar recognition for his theories of relativity).

The wave–particle duality notion was extended to electrons (particles surrounding the atomic nucleus) in 1924, by Louis de Broglie. De Broglie suggested that they might also be viewed, in some instances, as waves. In 1926, Erwin Schrodinger developed a wave equation for the electron, similar to Maxwell's equations for light. The classical view of matter made up of solid particles, which absorbed and emitted energy in continuous waves, was finally replaced by a strange new physics that accepted particles as waves, and waves as particles.

The essence of this quantum strangeness is conveyed by the 'two-slit experiment'.[14] This experiment has been carried out many times using photons, electrons or other sub-atomic 'particles', and sometimes with more than two slits, in the form of a diffraction grating or regularly spaced atoms in a crystal (from which X-rays or electrons can be bounced). In its simplest form, the experiment involves firing electrons at a screen with two small holes in it. At the other side of this screen, some form of detector screen is placed to record what happens when the electrons pass through the holes.

The set-up is similar to Young's two-slit experiment for light, which demonstrated the wave-like nature of light, from the interference pattern of the waves on the second screen. When waves go through the two slits, each of the slits becomes a new source of waves, thus giving rise to two new sets of waves which interfere with one another. Some of the waves cancel each other out, while others reinforce each other. In the case of light, this leads to a discernible interference pattern of bright and dark bands on the detector screen.

Using this experimental set-up, the wave-like nature of electrons can be demonstrated. Electron waves interfere with one another, in the same manner as light waves. The flashes on the detector that mark the arrival of individual electrons form bright stripes separated by dark regions. The electrons appear to behave like waves as they go through the holes, and then to coalesce into particles when they hit the detector screen.

We can interpret this part of the experiment in terms of the wave–particle duality, but what happens when we fire only one electron at a time in the direction of the experimental apparatus? When the electron passes through one of the slits, you observe a flash on the detector screen. Each time a flash occurs its position on the screen is recorded, and somewhat at odds with classical expectations, these flashes slowly build up to give the same diffraction pattern as before. Each individual electron has somehow behaved like a wave, 'interfering with itself'. Alternatively, the electrons have interfered with the 'memory' of each other (it is as though each electron is influenced by the path of the previous one), to produce the diffraction pattern.

It appears as though each electron goes through both slits simultaneously, which, to say the least, is strange. If we place additional detectors to note which slit the electron goes through, however, we find something even more strange. The detectors record the electrons as going through one slit or the other, and when we fire large numbers of them together at the apparatus, we find that we no longer get the diffraction pattern. The electrons no longer behave like waves. When we try to monitor their passage through the slits, they respond only as particles.

This has very deep implications. Not only is the idea of the existence of anything 'solid' called into question, but also it seems that the observer can no longer be separated from the observed. The observer is an integral part of the experiment. What we choose to observe will play a crucial role in what happens (our attempt to observe the electrons in the two-slit experiment had the effect of changing previous wave-like behaviour into particle-like behaviour). We cannot assume an 'objective' reality, which exists apart from our experience of it. It is not possible to observe something without changing it. We cannot even be sure of what is happening (according to Heisenberg's 'uncertainty principle', the more accurately we try to measure the position of a particle, the less accurately we can measure its speed, and vice versa). Consequently, at the sub-atomic level, we must abandon our attempts at predicting events with any certainty, and rely purely on statistical calculations to provide us with information on the probability of an event occurring.

Yet another piece of quantum strangeness arises from the Einstein–Podolsky–Rosen (EPR) paradox. This is the surprising consequence of quantum theory that once two systems (a pair of photons, for example) have interacted with each other, then a measurement on one of these systems can produce an instantaneous change in the state of the other system (in terms of direction of spin), even if they are by then widely separated from one another.[15] In other words, it suggests the possibility of non-local effects. Interference with a system in one part of the universe can produce a simultaneous effect on a system in another remote part of the universe.

Various interpretations have been placed upon these mysterious experimental findings, some of which are as strange as the findings themselves. One way of conceptualizing the quantum world is via the Schrodinger 'wave function'. The 'wave' is purely a mathematical concept, which can be applied in the calculation of probabilities of where an electron is going to turn up at any given moment of observation. When we 'look' at the electron (with the assistance of a particle detector), or attempt to measure it in some way, the wave function is said to 'collapse'. At that instant, we can tell the position of the electron. As soon as we stop looking, the wave function spreads out again, to its original form, and interferes with the wave functions of other electrons (or even with itself). The collapse of the wave function has a precise mathematical significance in quantum physics, and is the equivalent of saying that we can know where things are only when we are actually looking at them.[16]

Schrodinger's wave function is not so strange in itself, but the 'many-worlds' interpretation which is sometimes applied to it is, perhaps, stranger than science fiction. According to this view, when Schrodinger's wave collapses (at the instant of observation), the world splits up into many worlds. Each of the possible outcomes that could have occurred, as a result of our measurement or observation, does occur. Although we are only aware of the occurrence of one of these possibilities in our world, the others occur simultaneously in these other co-existing worlds, of which we are unaware. We are all the time being repeatedly cloned to carry on separate lives in the many worlds into which this world is continually splitting. So, if you did the football pools last week and lost, don't worry about it. You won and became a millionaire in some other universe! Whilst it is claimed that this theory belongs more to the 'Gee-Whizz' school of thought than to mainstream science, it is a view that is nevertheless popular with a number of respectable physicists.[17] It also fits the experimental findings as well as any other theory, with the advantage of providing a simpler explanation,[18] and it can apparently be upheld mathematically.[19]

Heinz Pagels includes the 'many worlds' interpretation along with three other major contenders in his analysis of what he calls the 'reality marketplace'.[20] One of these is the possibility that, to understand quantum physics, we will simply have to give up our adherence to Boolean logic (modern logic based on Boolean algebra) in the same way that we had to give up our adherence to Euclidean geometry (because of its two-dimensional limitations) to understand Einstein's relativity. This would be replaced by some new kind of quantum logic. The other two contenders are, however, the most popular. They are the 'objective reality' and 'local reality' (or Copenhagen) interpretations.

The 'objective reality' view suggests that the world exists independently of our knowledge of it, and that some day we will discover how to go beyond quantum theory in order to restore determinism. We are merely at a stage of ignorance, and our theories are incomplete. This interpretation accepts non-local instantaneous interactions (such as might take place in telepathy), and is, therefore, popular with mystics and occultists. It is consistent with the view that everything is connected to everything else in the universe.

The 'local reality' or Copenhagen interpretation, on the other hand, dismisses non-local causality as something that is only apparent. This interpretation is based on Heisenberg's 'uncertainty principle' and Bohr's 'principle of complementarity' (the principle that alternative and mutually exclusive descriptions are possible for dynamic systems[21]), and is the one that appeals most to mainstream physicists. The Copenhagen interpretation retains the internal consistency of quantum theory, but at the price of renouncing determinism and objectivity.[22] Reality is a matter of choice. Pagels sums it up as follows:

> The house of God that plays dice has many rooms. We can live in only one room at a time, but it is the whole house that is reality.[23]

The reference to God's dice-playing reflects both the non-determinist aspect of the Copenhagen interpretation and Einstein's oft-quoted comment ('God does not play dice') on this particular implication of quantum theory, which he did not like.

Whether we choose the reality shared by the mystics, the reality preferred by mainstream physicists, the seemingly strange reality of 'many worlds', or a reality involving an entirely new quantum logic, one thing is certain – we can no longer cling to our old ways of thinking about the world. This becomes even more evident when we consider Einstein's theories of relativity.

iii) Einstein's World

> Newton forgive me. You found the only way that, in your day, was at all possible for a man of the highest powers of intellect and creativity. The concepts that you created still dominate the way we think in physics, although we now know that they must be replaced by others farther removed from the sphere of immediate experience if we want to try for a more profound understanding of the way things are interrelated.
>
> — *Albert Einstein*[24]

Around the same time that quantum theory was forcing physicists to review their conceptions of reality at the level of the very small, relativity was stretching their imaginations in the world of the very large. In the same year that Einstein made his major contribution to quantum theory, he published another bombshell in the form of the special theory of relativity. The most famous aspect of this theory is, undoubtedly, the formula $E = mc^2$ (where c is the velocity of light), which reveals that mass and energy are merely two different and interchangeable forms of the same thing (thereby explaining where the heat and light energy radiated by stars comes from, and at the same time leading to the creation of the atomic bomb). There are, however, a number of other important aspects, which are more central to the theory.

If you are driving along a road at thirty miles per hour and you observe in the distance an oncoming car travelling at a speed of forty miles per hour, at what velocity would this vehicle be approaching you? – seventy miles per hour, of course. Now imagine travelling through space at a speed of 100,000 miles per second directly towards a (relatively) stationary source of light. Given that the speed of light (in empty space) is 186,000 miles per second, at what velocity should the light be reaching us? Suppose that we are moving directly away from the light source, what velocity should we now measure for the light as it reaches us? Contrary to what one might expect, the velocity of light remains constant irrespective of our motion relative to it. It will always reach our eyes at 186,000 miles per second, irrespective of whether we move towards the light source, whether we move away from it, whether we stand still, or whether it moves away from or towards us. This was the, apparently, paradoxical finding of the Michelson–Morley experiment.

According to classical physics, the speed of light should appear to change depending on the motion of the observer.

In the special theory of relativity, the speed of light becomes absolute, and the Michelson–Morley paradox is thus resolved. Regardless of the motion of its source, light always moves through empty space with the same constant speed. It is space and time that are relative, and not the speed of light. The concepts of absolute space and time have no meaning.[25]

If the speed of light as measured by an observer in motion relative to a light source is the same as that measured by an observer at rest relative to a light source, then the measuring instruments themselves must somehow change with the frame of reference, so that the speed of light always appears to be the same (remember that speed = space/time). In other words, to an observer at rest, a moving rod must change its length, and a moving clock must change its rate. At the same time, to the observer travelling along with the moving rod and clock, there is no apparent change in either the length of the rod or the rate of the clock.[26]

The time that you see on your own watch is your 'proper' (one's own) time, and the time that you see on the watch of the person moving past you is 'relative' time (it appears to you – although not to the other person – to be running more slowly than your watch). Similarly, the length of the measuring rod in your hand is its 'proper' length, and the length of the rod in the moving person's hand is the 'relative' length (which appears to you – although not to the other person – to be shorter). Furthermore, from the point of view of the person moving past you, he is at rest, you are moving, and the situation is reversed.

This aspect of the special theory gives rise to a phenomenon in physics, known as the Twin Paradox. If one twin goes on a space voyage while the other one remains on earth, his time will slow down relative to his brother's proper time on earth. When he returns, he will therefore be younger than his brother (it can be shown that he has actually aged less, when non-uniform motion is taken into account[27]). A similar situation arises when we fly on an aeroplane. Space and time shrinkage leads to our watches slowing down and to us getting thinner (although we also get heavier). The differences, however, are too minute for us to notice. The speed of the fastest aeroplane is very small compared with the speed of light. If we were able to travel at the speed of light, time would stand still, we would become invisible, and our mass would be infinite.

Not only are space and time not absolute or universal, but they are also, according to the special theory, inseparable. Most of us think (as did Newton) that space and time are separate, because that is the way we think that we experience them. We feel that we can control our position in three-dimensional space, but can do nothing about our forward movement in one-dimensional time. Whether or not we can do anything about the 'arrow of time' is another matter, but, in any case, Einstein argues that it is preferable to think in terms of a four-dimensional space–time continuum – a static picture of reality, which contains the past, present and future together, within a single frame of reference.

The special theory has been verified many times by experiments in high energy particle physics. Indeed, so thoroughly has it been confirmed by experiment that it would be hard to find a physicist today who doubts the theory's soundness.[28] In one dramatic experiment outside the laboratory, four of the most accurate atomic clocks available were flown around the world, in both easterly and westerly directions. At the end of the flight, they were found to be slightly behind their stationary, earthbound counterparts with which they had been synchronized at the start of the experiment.[29]

The Newtonian assumptions of universal time, a space that was independent of time, and an absolute, stationary frame of reference in space (the ether) were all shattered by the special theory of relativity. Added to this were the assertions that the speed of light must remain constant, that it is impossible to travel faster than the speed of light, and that mass and energy are merely two names for the same thing.

Despite its brilliance, the special theory had one major limitation – it applied only to uniform motion (motion at a constant speed). Einstein wanted a theory that encompassed all motion, including acceleration and deceleration. Ten years later (in 1915), he formulated just such a theory. He called it the general theory of relativity, because it applied to all motion (the special theory was so-called because it applied only to a special form of motion).

Martin Gardner describes the arrival of Einstein's general theory as follows:

> It came into the scientific world with something like the same effect that the new dance craze, the twist, invaded in 1962 the ballrooms of the United States. Einstein had given a new twist to the ancient dance rhythms of time and space. In a surprisingly short time every physicist in the world was either dancing the new twist, expressing shocked horror over it, or complaining that he was too old to learn.[30]

In one of Einstein's famous thought experiments (often referred to in explanations of the general theory), an elevator is pulled up through space with constantly increasing speed. If this acceleration is uniform, and exactly the same as the acceleration with which objects fall to the earth, then whoever is inside the elevator will believe themselves to be in a gravitational field exactly like the earth's. Similarly, in a falling elevator, inside the earth's gravitational field, the downward acceleration would completely eliminate the effect of gravity inside the elevator.

Einstein grasped that the effect of gravity was equivalent to acceleration, and vice versa. In doing so, he was able to extend his special theory to a general one that covered non-uniform, as well as uniform, motion. The principle of equivalence makes possible the view that all motion, including accelerated motion, is relative. All the laws of nature are the same with respect to any observer, and there is no experiment of any sort by which an observer in any sort of motion can prove whether he is moving or at rest. As Martin Gardner, with typical humour, puts it:

> Do the heavens revolve or does the earth rotate? The question is meaningless. A waitress might just as sensibly ask a customer if he wanted ice cream on top of his pie or the pie placed under his ice cream.[31]

Just as uniform motion slows the speed of time, so does non-uniform motion. As gravity is the equivalent of non-uniform motion, it also slows time. An interesting effect of this is that the top of your head is older than your feet. The speed of time at your feet has been calculated to be about 0.0000000000001 per cent less than the speed of time at your head, if you are six feet tall (and standing up).[32] If you live at the top of a mountain, you will, therefore, age more quickly than someone living at sea level. This effect has been demonstrated by placing atomic clocks at the top and bottom of a water tower. The clock at the bottom (with more gravity acting upon it due to its greater proximity to the earth) was found to run slower than the one at the top.[33]

Gravity (or non-uniform motion) also has the effect of bending light. Thus, the light reaching our eyes from a distant star may be deflected by the motion (or gravitational fields) of intervening bodies, such as other stars or planets. According to the general theory, the space–time continuum becomes warped by the presence of material objects. It is this distortion of the space–time continuum, by the presence of matter, that gives rise to what we perceive as the 'force' of gravity. There really is no force. Objects (including the photons in light) are simply following a path of least resistance, which is the equivalent of a straight line through space–time. When a planet, a beam of light, or any other object, moves near a large mass (and into a gravitational field, in our usual three-dimensional universe conception), its path bends along the line of least resistance.[34]

In four-dimensional space–time terms, the motion of the planets is not due to a gravitational 'force', as was claimed by Newton. This 'force' is simply a distortion in the space–time continuum. The planets orbit the sun simply because this is the easiest way for them to move in the space–time continuum in which they find themselves.[35]

This notion of four-dimensional space–time is impossible for us to conceptualize within our normal three-dimensional frame of reference. Whilst physicists can use mathematics to work with an unlimited number of dimensions, it can be very difficult for them to translate some of their ideas into a non-mathematical language. The problem of space–time can be tackled by thinking of a two-dimensional elastic surface, such as a rubber sheet.[36] If you dump a heavy bowling ball into the middle of the sheet, it bends, in the same way that space–time is bent by matter. Any object moving near the bowling ball will be 'pulled' down towards it by the bend in the sheet. This analogy is used to explain gravity within Einstein's model. However, this type of analogy leads one to think in terms of a space warp alone giving rise to gravity, thereby leaving out the importance of time, which can, by itself, explain gravity (it can be shown that gravity is caused by slow time, and not the other way around, although it is, of course, easier for us to think of time being influenced by a gravitational force).

Irrespective of any conceptual difficulties that Einstein's space–time and the link with gravity might pose for the non-physicist, the general theory of relativity is widely accepted as the best available model of the universe on a large scale, and its predictions have been borne out by a number of astronomical observations. The way that Mercury orbits the sun, the deflection of light from distant stars, and the longer wavelength (slower frequency) of radiation from elements found in sunlight, all provide evidence in favour of the general theory.[37]

The essence of what Einstein is telling us is this – reality is something that we can never fully comprehend,[38] but whatever it is, each of us interprets and experiences it in our own unique way from our individual frame of reference. Even time and distance, which most of us take to be absolute and universal, are relative to one's frame of reference and are experienced differently by everyone. What we normally perceive to be a force – the force of gravity – is not really a force at all. The objects that we see around us are, more accurately, forms of energy. There is no difference between matter and energy – they can be converted into each other.

The world that we live in is much stranger than most of us think. Look around you, what do you see? You see different parts of the past – the light from objects furthest away in your field of vision takes longest to reach you. What does your friend, standing beside you, see? Your friend sees other parts of the past. Now, suppose you start to walk away from your friend, and as you walk away, you throw a ball up into the air. You and your friend will observe the ball to be of different sizes, and to take different times to come back down again. Look at the night sky, what do you see? Again, different parts of the past, but not only do you see stars as they were at different times in history, you also observe them to be located in parts of space where they never were (the light from them, on its way to your eyes, will be bent by space–time curvature or, if you prefer the term, gravitational fields).

Fortunately (for Newton and the rest of us), we can get by with our old ideas of separate three-dimensional space and unidirectional time. This is because the time and space differences that we are talking about, in relativity, are minute and hence insignificant in our everyday world. They do not take on anything approaching significant proportions until we take our measurements into the macroscopic realm of the universe (or approach speeds in the region of 186,000 miles per second). The same applies to the seemingly strange world of quantum theory. It is only when we attempt to measure the sub-microscopic world of the atom that we encounter unusual aspects of reality that are not normally apparent in the world that we have come to know with the help of our Newtonian conceptualizations.

Most of us do not have to worry too much about the world of the very big or the world of the very small. We can muddle along contentedly with our old ways of seeing. The new physics, however, is asking us to stretch our imaginations, to broaden our range of perception, to adopt new models of reality, to see the world through new eyes, and to improve our understanding of it. It also points to an intimate relationship between self (the observer) and reality (the observed). It is no longer possible to keep these concepts separate.

iv) The World of the New Generation

The formulation of a single, ultimate theory that would explain the existence of all matter, all energy, and all the forces of nature was Einstein's dream.[39] It was a dream that he did not, of course, realize, but a new generation of physicists has taken over the quest. Some of them (Stephen Hawking, for example) believe that they are now very close to the unification of quantum theory and general relativity in a 'theory of everything'.[40]

One reason for Einstein's failure to produce the ultimate theory was his disregard of nuclear forces.[41] He concentrated his efforts on the unification of only two of nature's basic forces (electromagnetism and gravity) and ignored the other two: the strong force, which is thought to bind quarks together into the protons and neutrons that make up the atomic nucleus, and the weak force, which is seen to be responsible for certain kinds of radioactive decay.

Modern physicists explain the strong, weak, and electromagnetic forces in terms of quantum physics, and the force of gravity in terms of general relativity. The three forces incorporated into quantum theory are seen to be transmitted by packets (or *quanta*) of energy, called bosons, that behave both like particles and like waves (for example, the photon is the boson for light and other electromagnetic phenomena). Elementary particles of matter exchange energy by tossing bosons between each other in a kind of subatomic 'game of catch'.

The mathematical similarities between theories describing these forces have led theorists to suspect that they are descendants of a simpler, unified force that existed in the earliest moments of the universe.[42] They hope to find evidence for this primeval force by recreating, in giant accelerators, some of the high-energy conditions that would have existed in the early universe.

The electromagnetic and weak forces have already been unified in a now fairly well established 'electroweak' theory. According to this theory, at a temperature of about 10^{15} degrees (about the current limit for direct experimentation in particle accelerators) the four fundamental forces become three, with the electromagnetic force and the weak nuclear force merging in identity.[43]

Attempts have been made to extend this unification to incorporate the strong force in various 'grand unification theories' (GUTs), and even more ambitious attempts have been made to unify all four forces in 'theories of everything' (TOEs). Such theories still await experimental evidence to support them, due to the extremely high energies that would be required to test them. It is thought that the strong force would merge with the electromagnetic–weak force at 10^{27} degrees, and that at 10^{32} degrees gravity would merge with the electromagnetic–weak–strong force to produce a single, unified superforce.[44]

Whether or not one of these TOEs eventually becomes established as a complete and universally accepted unified theory, it would not mean that we would be able to predict events in general. As Hawking points out, the 'uncertainty principle' would continue to set a limit on our powers of prediction, and, in any case, we would not be able to solve the equations of the theory exactly, except in very simple situations.[45]

The point, however, is not whether we will eventually arrive at a complete understanding of the universe. The answer to that, as I will argue later, has to be 'No'. What I am trying to convey is that there are indications, coming from the new physics, to suggest that nature has an underlying unity – a unity that is not merely related to its common origin,[46] but leads us to suppose that everything is still connected to everything else, as it was in the beginning.

Whilst the modern physicist's world remains predominantly fragmented, it is moving away from the notion that we can separate ourselves from the rest of the world. It is moving away from the illusion of separateness.

The distinction between 'it' and 'not it' is becoming increasingly blurred. The further we attempt to stretch the bounds of our knowledge, the more apparent it becomes that separateness is an illusion. When we delve into the world of the very small, we are unable to separate ourselves from the objects of our experiments; the 'particles' that we try to measure take on the form of waves; the 'particles' that we had regarded as separate turn out to be interconnected; matter and energy become interchangeable. When we examine the world of the very large, we find we can no longer distinguish between space and time, or even between gravity and time.

What we tend to think of as space, time, gravity (or other 'fundamental' forces), matter, energy, or even consciousness – they are impossible to distinguish between, for they are all one. The dividing lines that were drawn between them served science in its past understanding of the universe. As science pushes this understanding to new limits, however, the lines begin to disappear.

CHAPTER

Through The Looking Glass

As indicated in the previous chapter, modern physics suggests a close relationship between the self and 'external' reality, even though most of us still perceive a separate self with our Newtonian conceptions of reality (the latest ideas in science always take a while to filter through – even to other scientists).

Quantum mechanics forces us to recognize that the observer and the observed can no longer be viewed as independent entities. Consciousness and the physical world cannot be kept apart. It is impossible to explain the workings of our universe without including consciousness (or the processes of observation) somewhere in the equation. It is this part of the equation that I will now turn to in an attempt to produce the beginnings of a unified theory embracing both physics and psychology. These two fundamental sciences must come together to bring the dream of the theoretical physicist closer to reality. The explainer must be included in the explained, otherwise not everything is explained (although I will argue later that science can never explain everything).

In an attempt to stretch scientific theory to its current limits, I propose to bring the explainer and the explained together by relating our sense of self to our sense of the external world.

THE LOOKING-GLASS WORLD

Each to each a looking glass
reflects the other that doth pass
— *Charles Cooley*[1]

Look in the mirror. What do you see? Look at the world. What do you see? Look at your friend; look at a stranger; look at a tree; look at a stone. What you see is you. Or to be more precise, what you see is a reflection of various aspects of the self. Why else should the world appear different to each and every one of us? The world that we know and experience is a reflection of the self.

In 1902, Charles Cooley declared that 'self and society are twin born . . . and the notion of a separate and independent ego is an illusion'.[2] Self and society mutually define each other, acting as points of reference for one another. The concept of self is influenced by how we think others see us.[3] As we interact with those around us, we obtain feedback on how they see us. Our interpretation of the reactions of others, to the things we do and say, shapes our view of ourselves. Hence, we see ourselves in the 'looking-glass' of society. Cooley coined the term 'looking-glass self' to refer to this phenomenon.

In my version of the looking-glass self, I am taking the concept a bit further – to include everything, in fact. I am also turning it around. The entire world that we see and experience is a reflection of self, so what we live in is a *looking-glass world*.

When you acquire new information from the external world, you are merely building up associations around the self. The more of the external world you encounter, then the more of these associations you will accumulate in the form of knowledge. No matter how much of this worldly knowledge you acquire, however, it will always remain knowledge in relation to *you* or in relation to *your* systems of communication or logic. You can never get away from you in your perception of the world. Even when you think you are taking the view of another, you are only taking the view of the other from *your* point of view.

Think for a moment how you view a stone. You do not look at it from the stone's point of view. You see a stone in terms of its relation to *you* – it may make up part of your house or provide you with a potential weapon. You may also think of it as having certain properties, such as a particular colour or shape. These properties are derived from the classification systems that we have learned within our particular society. They are simply codes, however, that we employ for communication purposes (although colour and shape may take on associations drawn from other objects, where they have in some way played a key role in relation to self). For all we know, my black could be your white, or your yellow my red. We have agreed only on the code, but not necessarily on the sensation. Just because we all agree to call grass green does not necessarily mean that we all perceive it as the same colour.

Language is, of course, a useful tool for classifying and communicating our perceptions. We can also use it to store ideas that have no personal meaning for us (which come in handy when playing *Trivial Pursuit*), but our basic conception of the world 'out there' runs deeper than that. When we live for the self (and I have argued that most of us do), then non-self can have little meaning outside its relation to self. I will perceive non-self (the world) in terms of its function for self (I, me, mine, and so on). It must surely follow that my perception of self will be intimately related to my perception of non-self. My perception of one will mirror my perception of the other.

Research on the relationship between our perceptions of self and others provides some evidence for this. Psychologists have noted that evaluations, judgements, predictions and inferences about a particular quality in other people often depend on the individual's own position relative to that quality.[4] They have identified three main ways in which our view of ourselves plays a role in our perception of other people.

Firstly, it has been suggested that we use our perception of self to fill information gaps on others when judgements are required on the basis of inadequate information – a phenomenon referred to as 'self-projection'.[5] Frequently we assume that others have or should have similar attitudes, interests and abilities as ourselves. We are not always aware that we are doing this, however, and can find ourselves providing descriptions of other people that say more about ourselves than they do about the people we are trying to describe. It was on this basis that the so-called 'projective' techniques, such as the ink-blot test (which asked people to describe a variety of 'ink-blot' shapes, in the hope that this would convey something about their personality) were formulated. Although these tests were eventually criticized because nobody could agree on how to interpret the results, they are evidence of the strongly held view that much of the self is projected into descriptions of non-self.

Secondly, it has been suggested that we direct our perceptual processes in a self-serving manner to maintain or enhance self-esteem – a phenomenon referred to as 'self-image bias'.[6] We tend to pay more attention to areas of life where we feel we are likely to attain some measure of success.

Areas of potential failure do not normally feature prominently in our interests and motives. If you can't dance, you may prefer to talk about football.

Thirdly, the self is seen to serve as a frame of reference or baseline against which relevant information about others is compared and contrasted. This tendency to employ the self as a focal point for incoming information is referred to as 'egocentricity'.[7] Whether you judge a person to be rich, fit or competent in some area may depend on your own position in whatever it is you happen to be judging. This is not the same thing as 'self-projection'. In the case of 'egocentricity', we are deliberately placing the target in some position on a scale relative to our own position on that same scale. If, for example, a person's average score at ten-pin bowling is 120, I will perceive her to be 'good' at the game if my average is only 80. However, if my average is 160, then I might perceive her to be a 'poor' bowler. The same line of argument may be applied to income and perceived social status. As Charles Cooley argued, self and society mutually define each other, acting as points of reference for one another.[8] Not only is the concept of self shaped by how we think others see us (as in Cooley's 'looking-glass self'), but our perception of others is shaped by our concept of self.

In order to test the relationship between self and other-perception, I asked 233 first-year psychology students, whom I was meeting for the first time, to describe themselves and to describe me.[9] I found a very strong relationship between their perception of themselves and their perception of me. Those who described themselves as happy were more likely to see me as being happy. If troubled by worry, they were more likely to see me as being troubled in the same way. It seems that a person's description of someone else may tell you more about him than it does about the person he is supposed to be describing.

In another experiment, I deliberately manipulated students' self-esteem by telling them they had done well or poorly on a bogus 'IQ Test'.[10] They were then asked to watch a film and to describe the speaker in the film afterwards. Those who thought they had done poorly in the test were less likely to mention ability, in describing the speaker, than were the group who thought they had done well. Once again, perception of self appeared to play a central role in the perception of someone else.

From my own work on the relationship between self and other-perception, I am left in no doubt that all the things we say about other people and the way we treat them stem more from our view of ourselves than from any objective assessment of those others. My first suspicions of this were aroused in a study of unemployed people's perceptions of themselves and others.[11]

As one might expect, the unemployed see themselves in a more negative light than they see others. For example, they feel that they are more likely to suffer from depression and problems of ill-health than those in jobs. However, they also hold a more negative view of the entire adult population than the view held by the employed. In other words, their negative view of themselves is, to some extent, projected onto others.

It was this finding that disturbed me most and pushed me towards further research on the relationship between self and other-perception. It bothered me (and still does) to think that if you lower a person's self-esteem by taking away her job, or by telling her in some other way that she has in some sense failed, then not only does her view of herself become depressed, but also her view of the entire world and its possibilities becomes depressed.

It is small wonder that so many of us do little else but complain about the world around us and the people in it. Much of this negative view of the world stems from our creation of a competitive social system which inevitably brands most of us failures in some sense. In an economic system that requires a certain level of unemployment, failure is inevitable. In an education system that grades children as one would grade eggs, failure is inevitable. The more we encourage competition, the more we create failure. With so much failure in our lives, how can we think highly of ourselves or our world?

The point of the argument, however, is not to knock the existing political system of the West and to promote some form of substitute. All political systems have their strengths and weaknesses and will likely gain from a merger of some sort in the future. What I really want to examine here, however, is the relationship between individual consciousness and the external reality perceived by the individual. The point that I want to make, then, is this – the external world that each of us perceives is simply a reflection of our internal world or self.

What we see in other people is inextricably related to what we see and experience in ourselves. When you judge others on any quality, you judge yourself. The rank that you give to others in your rating of them will determine your own ranking. When you describe others, you describe yourself. Your description will inevitably contain things that matter to you, though not necessarily things that matter to the person you are describing. When you evaluate a person's behaviour as good or bad, you do so in relation to what is good or bad for you, and not what is good or bad for them. When you look at others, you look at yourself.

SPACE, TIME AND SELF

It is easy enough to put forward an idea such as the *looking-glass world*, and to argue that, in some way, our conceptions of 'internal' and 'external' reality reflect each other. It is more difficult to take the idea further and to develop it into a model that brings together the 'internal' reality of the psychologist and the 'external' reality of the physicist.

Returning to the world of quantum physics presented earlier, we may take as our starting point the role of the participating observer in experimental outcomes. We noticed that the actions of the observer had an important part to play in the outcome. The current state of any quantum system can be described by the Schrodinger wave-function which allows for an infinite number of potential outcomes upon disturbance of the system. According to the Copenhagen interpretation, as soon as the observer attempts to measure the system, the wave-function collapses and one of the potential outcomes is realized. In the many-worlds interpretation, the wave-function does not collapse and all outcomes are realized (in different universes). In the Copenhagen interpretation, the principle of complementarity allows us to switch from a wave view to a particle view. By not making this switch in absolute frames of reference, one is left with an infinite number of outcomes and hence an infinite number of worlds.

Einstein, in his theory of relativity, has already demonstrated that everything is relative to the observer's frame of reference. For him, that frame of reference was the observer's location in space and time ('external' reality). I want to extend the frame of reference to include mind (the observer's 'internal' reality). In this way, not only can fundamental concepts from psychology and physics be brought together, but aspects of quantum theory and relativity can also be subsumed within the same model.

What I am proposing is an extension of the basic idea behind relativity in an attempt to account for both mind and matter in a single theory. In so doing, I hope to bring together the participating observer and the object of observation. Instead of a reality consisting of four dimensions (three of space, and one of time), I suggest that we consider a reality consisting of seven dimensions – three of space, one of time, and three of mind. The number of dimensions of mind that are built into the model is not important. I have suggested three, but I could just as easily postulate one, two, four or five. What is important is the integration of mind into the space–time continuum (events occur not only in space–time, but also in mind).

In this view of the world, the dream is no less real than the dreamer, and a desk is no less real than the hypothesized electrons it contains. Concepts such as objectivity and subjectivity become obsolete as we move to a higher (in the sense that it is more complete) level of explanation. The distinctions between mind and matter and between the subjective reality of the observer and the objective reality of the external world disappear in this seven-dimensional view in the same way that the distinction between time and space disappears in Einstein's four-dimensional view. Space–time is extended to become space–time–mind.

In addition to seeing or measuring things in an external world of space and time, we also experience them mentally in some way. If we confine ourselves to a space–time model that accounts for the 'external' part of an event we believe to be taking place independently of our observations, then not only do we hold a view that runs counter to the findings of quantum physics (that the observer and the observed are not independent of one another), but we also leave out an obviously important part of the event (the observer's mind).

As the observer's mind is applied to the formulation of a theory to account for what is happening 'out there', then any theory that includes mind should, to some extent, encompass theory formulation within the theory. In other words, it should be reflexive. It should account for itself in addition to accounting for other theories. By bringing mind into the picture, I believe that we can, to a large extent, achieve this.

THE DIMENSIONS OF MIND

The three dimensions of mind that I propose to add are those of *consciousness* (which roughly equates with cognition), *feeling* (which equates with affect), and what I shall call *focus* (which relates to motivation). In a way, they reflect the three dimensions of space, in that consciousness can be construed in terms of low–high awareness (*height*), feeling can be thought of in terms of a sense of closeness to something along a spectrum of integration–alienation (*depth*), and focus refers to *breadth* of interest or attention.

The three dimensions of mind represent the mind of the observer. The three dimensions of space represent what we have come to regard as the external world. The dimension of time embraces both the observer and the observed, and represents process or change. The relationship between mind and space may be viewed as isomorphic, and generated by the mirror of time (in that our perceptions of the 'internal' and 'external' worlds are generated by process or change, which is what time effectively is). This is similar to Jung's view of psychic and physical energy as two aspects of the same reality, with the world of matter appearing as a reflected image of the world of the psyche, and vice versa.[12]

Through the mirror of time, the pattern of life in space and in mind constantly changes. As with the concept of space–time, the seven dimensions of space–time–mind should be regarded as interconnected aspects of the same continuum. In short, they are inseparable.

Just as perception of the world is relative to the observer's position in space–time in relativity theory, so it is relative to the observer's position in space–time–mind in the proposed extension of relativity theory. As all interpretations of the world require an absolute frame of reference (that is, the observer must view reality from some point along the space–time–mind continuum), the removal of this absolute will lead to an infinite number of views, such as we encounter with the many-worlds interpretation. Ultimately, this interpretation is the most complete one. There *are* an infinite number of worlds for different locations in space, time and mind.

The many-worlds view, therefore, encompasses the whole of space, time and mind. To make sense of our world, however, we are forced to relate everything to some absolute frame of reference. This is what Einstein and Newton both did. Newton's frames of reference were absolute space and absolute time. Einstein combined these into a single absolute of space–time,[13] held together through the constancy of the speed of light (space and time are brought together in the concept of speed). I am suggesting a further step in the scientific process – absolute space–time–mind, with space–time itself becoming relative to the observer's position in mind.

I propose that we consider extending relativity theory to encompass the genesis of the theory itself. From this perspective, Einstein's theory becomes relative to his position on the space–time–mind continuum. He needed a frame of reference, and that frame of reference was provided by the constant c. Richard Gregory (who, in my view, stops just a fraction short of taking the audacious step I am now proposing) also points out the need for an absolute, and at the same time alerts us to this important point about Einstein's theory.

Einstein somehow inferred or guessed that if c were accepted as an absolute, then order could be made of the rest. The constants of physics are postulates that serve as keystones of theories. Without constants the

structure falls; without the structure, there is nothing
to support them as anything special . . . We may say
that Relativity Theory, which was born of seeking
objective truth by carrying out real or imaginary procedures, confirms, or at least is no exception to, the
notion that truth itself is relative: that knowledge
depends on assumptions or postulates that are taken
as absolute because without them we cannot, with
meaning, say or see.[14]

So while we might take a position of extreme relativism as
our starting point, and thereby account for the many-worlds
interpretation of quantum physics, it is necessary, from a
practical point of view (in order that the theory should have
some useful explanatory or predictive power) to establish a
frame of reference by appealing to some absolute.

In this proposed version of reality, Einstein's constant c is
replaced by a moving constant, representing that part of the
system that has been accepted on faith. The constant moves
as the level of analysis changes. The constant is whatever
article of faith the observer finds most useful for purposes of
explanation or prediction. For example, a theory in physics
may be built around the existence of 'atoms' – a concept
taken on faith. Instead of an implicit assumption within the
model, the assumption becomes explicit as a constant or
stated frame of reference, upon which all else is based.
Einstein's c therefore becomes only one of an infinite number
of possible constants, which may be drawn upon to provide
meaning.

At the higher levels of analysis, the constant may be
God's Will or Mill's Utilitarianism; at the lower physical
levels, it may still be c – until it is replaced by something
considered by scientists to be more useful. Whatever the
constant or frame of reference, it will represent an explicit

statement of an article of faith we have accepted from a higher level to fill the inevitable gap in our knowledge.

Schematically, the concept of extended relativity may be represented by one large complete circle (the whole) containing an infinite number of progressively smaller, concentric, incomplete circles (our models). The gap in each of the smaller circles is filled by the constant in the model (an article of faith borrowed from a larger circle). Any point can be chosen from an infinite number of points within the larger circle to represent a constant or frame of reference depending on the observer's position in space, time and mind (see diagram below).

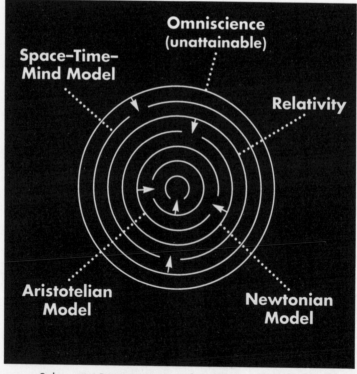

Schematic Representation of a 'Theory of Theories'

The present theory, then, may be thought of as a 'theory of theories', which includes itself in the model. The space–time–mind continuum is the 'absolute' that I have introduced as a frame of reference, around which the theory is constructed. The existence of a space–time–mind continuum cannot be proved from within the theory, so the theory is not complete. However, this is true of all theories, and this is the way that science makes its advances, moving *ad infinitum* from one incomplete circle to a larger, but still, incomplete circle, in 'paradigm shifts'.[15]

My proposed dimensions of mind require some development, but in their present raw form the three dimensions may be described briefly as follows:

i) The Dimension of Consciousness

The dimension of consciousness can be related to Schumacher's principle of adequateness, which asserts that we understand or are aware of only that which we are equipped to understand.[16] The body of knowledge and theory that we amass through science, learning and inheritance is what gives us our adequateness for understanding. The lower the level of consciousness, the less we can comprehend. Consciousness has, of course, developed to a higher level in humans than in animals, and to different levels in different individuals. Gurus, for example, are generally regarded to have a more fully developed consciousness than most people, and according to those who propose evolution of the consciousness we are all evolving towards this higher level.

ii) The Dimension of Feeling

The dimension of feeling can be related to Birch's aspects of alienation. He views humanity as being engaged in a search for wholeness, and currently in need of integration on a number of different levels.[17] These levels are self, society, our environment, and the 'whole scheme of things'. Our present life crises, Birch argues, stem from our lack of a sense of oneness with self, with others, with the world, and with the whole scheme of things – in a word, alienation. The dimension of feeling, then, ranges from alienation at one end to integration or love at the other. Whether or not humanity is evolving further along this dimension, in terms of an increased capacity for love, is a matter of debate, but there does seem to be something within us that impels us to strive towards integration.

Wilber's spectrum of consciousness appears to encompass both dimensions of consciousness and feeling.[18] The highest level of consciousness, according to this model, is the level of Mind, which is the absolute and ultimate reality of the universe (referred to variously as Brahman, Tao, Dharmakaya, Allah, or the Godhead). This is the level of consciousness that the mystic aspires to attain. The lowest level, the Shadow level, involves a sense of alienation from the self, with various undesirable parts of the self being rejected as contents of the Shadow. Different levels of consciousness correspond to different modes of knowing, and also to different modes of identity and feelings of alienation. The lower the level of consciousness, the greater the feelings of alienation.

iii) The Dimension of Focus

Finally, the dimension of focus can be related to Doise's levels of analysis, which refer to the different levels at which we attempt to capture reality through the use of models.[19] He identifies four of these levels – the intra-personal, inter-personal, positional (relating to social position), and ideological (involving belief systems, values, norms, and so on). Although the dimension of focus involves much more than these four levels, Doise's classification scheme contains the same basic idea.

We can focus on a very narrow range of reality – a cell, the self, or another individual – or we can widen our range of interest to encompass all of humanity (in, for example, a sociological or psychological theory), or even the entire universe (in a cosmological theory). Our position on the dimension of focus will depend on our motivation, on what aspect of reality we are trying to grasp. If we are primarily interested in our selves, then we will spend more time located on that part of the focal dimension. The holistic movement, generally, is asking us to widen our range of interest beyond our selves and to take account of a greater part of the whole in our thoughts, feelings and actions.

In an analogous manner to the expansion of the physical universe, mind is also expanding. Our range of consciousness, feeling and focus is growing. We know more, feel more, and have a wider range of interest than our ancestors (all stemming from the exponential growth in knowledge and corresponding increase in potential sources of stimulation and interest). There is now much more to understand, much more to perceive, and much more to do. Unless the 'arrow of time' changes direction, this trend will continue. We are, literally, becoming more broad-minded.

The observer's position in space–time–mind will determine his or her view of reality. All views of reality are, therefore, relative to that position. Each of us holds many different views of reality as we pass through time. In putting forward a particular model of the world, we try to increase the lifetime of some of our views, and influence the future views of others.

The theory presented above accepts the principle that 'everything is relative to everything else'. This itself is an absolute that cannot be proved from within the theory. My view is no more right or wrong than anybody else's, and all the 'evidence' I supply you with will not alter that, but if it serves you in any way – helps you to integrate existing knowledge, enables you to make some reliable prediction, helps you to extract some meaning from life, reduces your feelings of alienation, or gives you a sense of purpose – you will adopt it.

Below the level of God, there can be no absolute truth. At the human level, there can only be a great many relative truths. Like a ship passing land, we throw down the occasional anchor to get a better look, only to realize that our view of the land changes according to where we cast our anchor.

I have attempted to stretch science to its limits by bringing elements of physics and psychology together in a theory of extreme relativism. But even if such a theory were to offer us complete understanding, it would fail to provide the moral absolutes that we require to guide our behaviour. A complete scientific theory would tell us what we had to do in order to achieve certain objectives. It could not tell us whether or not those objectives were good or bad (except in relation to other objectives, which in turn would have to be measured against other objectives, and so on, *ad infinitum*).

In fact, the limits of science and any scientific theory are not only confined by a failure to provide moral absolutes. When stretched to its limits, science can offer no absolutes of any kind, except that which it borrows from outside its province. All absolutes must be accepted on faith, as they can neither be proved nor disproved within the theory to which they belong. In our search for a theory of everything, the best we can hope for is an internally consistent theory that explains everything that it sets out to explain, except for a small article of faith that it has borrowed from the infinity of mystery that lies outside the domain of science.

PART THREE

THE
MYSTICAL
UNIVERSE

RELIGION

Science cannot solve the ultimate mystery of nature. And that is because, in the last analysis, we ourselves are part of nature, and, therefore, part of the mystery that we are trying to solve.

— *Max Planck*[1]

In the previous chapter, I attempted to put together a synthesis of physics and psychology. The resultant theory still needs some work, but I feel that it at least demonstrates the potential for a 'high-level' scientific theory that can embrace all science. As I have already stated, it is not, by any stretch of the imagination, a complete theory, nor can it ever be. No scientific theory can explain everything. We need to look beyond science for a complete explanation, and for the meaning that we so desperately desire.

SCIENCE AND RELIGION

Science without religion is lame, religion without science is blind.

— *Albert Einstein*[2]

Religion and science are the two wings upon which
man's intelligence can soar into the heights.
— *'Abdu'l-Bahá*[3]

Despite all our scientific advances and our optimistic quest for
a scientific theory of everything, increasingly we feel that
something is missing. The truth is, as I have already
indicated, there *is* something missing, and there will always be
something missing, as long as we attempt to build our world-
view solely around science. The absolutes of science (should
they be Einstein's speed of light or Newton's space and time)
must be taken on faith in the same way that religious beliefs
are accepted. We can no more prove that the speed of light is
constant and unsurpassable than we can prove the existence
of God.

In a passage I have already quoted, Richard Gregory
points out that such absolutes are merely postulates that
serve as keystones for theories; we must draw assumptions
from outside the theory and accept them as absolute, because
'without them we cannot, with meaning, say or see'.[4] All
science, therefore, contains an element of incompleteness, in
that there will always be some part of any scientific theory
(at least one absolute) that cannot be proved from within
the theory.

Between 1910 and 1913, a monumental three-volume
work, in the form of *Principia Mathematica*, was produced by
Bertrand Russell and Alfred North Whitehead. Its goal was
to derive all mathematics from formal logic without any con-
tradictions. It claimed to be both complete and consistent in
its coverage of mathematics. This claim particularly bothered
the German mathematician, David Hilbert, who challenged
the world community of mathematicians to demonstrate rigorously that the system defined in *Principia Mathematica* was
both consistent and complete.[5]

In 1931, Kurt Godel responded to this challenge in a paper which showed that Russell and Whitehead's original aims (to provide a system of mathematics that was both complete and consistent) were illusory. Godel set out to prove that: a) within any system there are formally undecidable propositions; and b) that consistency cannot be formalized within the system. He demonstrated mathematically that no axiomatic system whatsoever could be produced that was complete, unless it was inconsistent.

Furthermore, the consistency of any formal system of logic cannot be proved from within the system. Proof of consistency requires justification from a meta-system.[6] In other words, there will always be some assumption present in the model that has been taken from a higher level system of logic. Everything within the model has, in effect, been built around this assumption, but there is nothing within the model itself that can prove or disprove the assumption. This applies to *all* models, and leads to an infinite regress of appeals for proof to higher systems.

Godel's Incompleteness Theorem suggests that it is impossible for science to ascertain any absolute truth or law of nature. This is a point that is stressed by Paul Davies, in his latest book *The Mind of God*.[7] He dismisses the possibility of a scientific theory of everything on the basis of Godel's theorem, and also reminds us of the fundamentally quantum nature of the world and its inherent indeterminism. He concludes that 'there will always remain some openness, some element of mystery, something unexplained'.[8]

Further evidence of the inevitable incompleteness of logical systems comes from the area of artificial intelligence, where Turing in England and Church working independently in America showed that no procedure could be devised to test every assertion in a logical system and demonstrate it to be either true or false.[9] In other words, at least one assertion must come from outside the system and cannot be tested from within the system. Roger Penrose draws on this point to support his argument against artificial intelligence.[10] Essentially, he argues that human thinking, through its use of insight and its access to 'God-given mathematical ideas', goes beyond formal logic.

The theorems of Godel, Turing and Church, clearly, have fundamental implications. On the basis of these theorems, Bronowski concludes that physicists searching for an all-embracing theory have set themselves an impossible goal.

> It follows in my view that the unwritten aim that the physical sciences have set themselves since Isaac Newton's time cannot be attained. The laws of nature cannot be formulated as an axiomatic, deductive, formal, and unambiguous system which is also complete. And if at any stage in scientific discovery the laws of nature did seem to make a complete system, then we should have to conclude that we had not got them right.[11]

Given that science can provide no absolute truths to guide us, and given that the nature of the world appears to be fundamentally indeterminate, is it not time that science looked to religion for help in its search for understanding and meaning? It should be recognized that we are not dealing simply with the *facts* of science and the *superstitions* of religion. Both involve faith and relative truth, and both have something to offer each other. Religion embraces the mystery that science can never pin down, while science embraces understanding that would otherwise remain a mystery. Religion can support science and give it direction ('science without religion is lame'), while science can help religion to remove the veils of dogma from its vision ('religion without science is blind').

For centuries science and religion have gone their separate ways, meeting occasionally only to do battle. The Catholic Church in Europe fought to hold on to its virtual monopoly on knowledge and beliefs, but the scientific revolution of the seventeenth century proved too strong to suppress. Science, in winning a number of important battles, eventually won the war. By the twentieth century, science had become the dominant force in the West, leading many people to view religion as an outmoded set of values and beliefs.[12] Science, to some extent, became the new road to salvation. It offered freedom, justice, harmony, improved living conditions, and even longer life, where religion could offer only oppression, injustice and conflict. This particular aspect of the demise of religion is highlighted by physicist Anjam Khursheed as follows:

> Religion . . . has often prided itself on the infallibility of its doctrines, making its beliefs exempt from revision and, at certain points in history, not hesitating to impose them by torture and burning at the stake. Because science has a method for choosing rationally between rival theories, it has progressed peacefully and brought together people of every nation, race and tradition in a harmonious quest for knowledge. Religion, however, has often clung to outmoded visions and has divided people against each other in a deafening quarrel between conflicting dogmas. It also stands accused of making false promises by speaking of eternal rewards for the faithful. According to some thinkers, these promises are best understood as instruments of social oppression by which ruling social elites retain the obedience of exploited classes and secure their resignation to inadequate earthly rewards.[13]

Our disillusionment with the Church (referred to in Chapter 2) and our reaction against its dogma and hypocrisy, may, however, have led us to rely too heavily on science as an alternative, instead of a complementary, 'way of seeing' our world. We now find that a scientifically oriented view of the universe cannot provide us with a wholly satisfactory alternative. Not only has it failed to provide the answers to everything in the physical world as promised at one time (when Lord Kelvin suggested that science had more or less finished its job[14]), but it has also led us to neglect the spiritual side of our nature and to focus more on the physical. This spiritual neglect now manifests itself in the social and psychological malaise that Jung warned us about,[15] and in the feeling of meaninglessness (referred to earlier) that many of us now experience.

The early promise of psychology, as a scientific approach that would replace religion in treating and understanding spiritual matters, has fallen flat somewhere along the secular road. The increase in mental illness and depressive reactions, such as suicide, in recent years is testimony enough to that. Approximately one out of every three or four people in our present society will require treatment at some time in their lives for some form of mental illness.[16] Over the past quarter of a century, the suicide rate among adolescents and young adults has increased almost tenfold, and there are now as many as 55,000 suicides every year in the United States alone.[17] Recent increases in the incidence of crime, divorce, drug abuse and alcohol abuse provide further evidence of a need to re-think our position.

It has even been claimed that the 'advances' of medical science have been greatly exaggerated.[18] The efficacy of its methods has recently been called into question, with more people dying from the adverse effects of drug-therapy than from road accidents and an increasing number of people being subjected to unnecessary surgery with sometimes fatal consequences.[19]

Indeed, the current problems within the fields of medicine and psychology have led a number of writers to talk in terms of 'crisis'[20] – a term that has also been applied to our educational, political and economic systems.[21] Sociologist Alvin Toffler sums up the situation:

> We find crisis in the welfare systems. Crisis in the postal systems. Crisis in the school systems. Crisis in the health-delivery systems. Crisis in the urban systems. Crisis in the international financial system. The nation-state itself is in crisis. The Second Wave value system is in crisis . . . Today we see millions desperately searching for their own shadows, devouring movies, plays, novels, and self-help books, no matter how obscure, that promise to help them locate their missing identities . . . They itch for change but are terrified by it.[22]

It seems that the rapid growth of science, and our desire to find an alternative road to salvation, led to unrealistic expectations. Some of us thought (and some of us still think) that it could provide the answer to everything. The increasing realization that it cannot live up to these expectations, and that we may have built a Tower of Babel,[23] is leading a growing number of scientists to talk in terms of crisis.

Ironically, theologians are now also talking in terms of crisis. Although the Jewish and Christian Churches have for a long time been worried about secularization and the decline in church attendance, they have only recently begun to recognize their failure to keep pace with modern thinking. Keith Ward outlines the crisis in Christianity as follows:

For some time it has become clear that the Christian faith is a faith in crisis. Since the Enlightenment its traditional claims have been successively undermined, until now there often seems to be a complete breakdown between faith and modern culture. Traditionalists try to pretend that the Enlightenment has never happened and those who seek new statements of belief are hampered by having to pay lip-service to apparently outworn doctrines, so as not to offend traditionalist believers. As a result, the vast majority of Western people have become religiously dispossessed, unable to accept traditional doctrines and unable to understand how revisionist theologies can be part of such traditions.[24]

Ward points out that the literal or infallibilist interpretation of the Bible is now being relinquished by modern theologians. The literal truth of historical narratives is no longer viewed as essential to an appreciation of the true function of religion, which is now seen to be the disclosure of ultimate value and meaning and the liberation of humanity from selfishness and frustration. He is optimistic about the future of religion, and suggests that a new religious phoenix will rise from the present ashes. This new spirituality will be tolerant of both variety and change, and will work together with the emerging new science to promote a vision of human wholeness and responsibility.[25]

To use the analogy of 'Abdu'l-Bahá (son of Bahá'u'lláh, founder of the Bahá'í Faith), we have attempted in the past to fly almost exclusively on one 'wing' or the other, and we must now learn to fly on both 'wings'. As Einstein indicated, we need to combine science with religion to give support and direction to both. This notion of complementarity between science and religion is elucidated further in the following statement, made by 'Abdu'l-Bahá:

There is no contradiction between true religion and science. When a religion is opposed to science it becomes mere superstition; that which is contrary to knowledge is ignorance.

How can a man believe to be a fact that which science has proved impossible? If he believes in spite of his reason, it is rather ignorant superstition than faith. The true principles of all religions are in conformity with the teachings of science.

The unity of God is logical, and this idea is not antagonistic to the conclusions arrived at by scientific study.

All religions teach that we must do good, that we must be generous, sincere, truthful, law-abiding, and faithful; all this is reasonable, and logically the only way in which humanity can progress.

All religious laws conform to reason, and are suited to the people for whom they were framed, and for the age in which they are to be obeyed.[26]

In his bestselling book, *The Tao of Physics*, physicist Fritjof Capra has already done much to demonstrate the existence of parallels between modern physics and the eastern religions of Hinduism, Buddhism and Taoism.[27] The essence of this similarity is their shared view of an interrelatedness and a fundamental unity of all things in the universe. Whilst this shows that science and religion need not necessarily be in conflict with one another, it still leaves a number of major religions out in the cold, not least those that predominate in the West. This is an imbalance that I hope to redress in my attempt to draw the major religions into a scientific–religious synthesis, although I believe that this has, to a large extent, already been done within the framework provided by Bahá'u'lláh over a century ago – a point I will return to later.

I have already argued that science cannot go beyond incomplete models, and that it ultimately depends on an element of faith. In the diagram on p. 104, the advance of science was depicted as a series of incomplete circles (of finite size), moving outward towards a complete circle (of infinite size), which can never be reached. The incomplete circles represent incomplete scientific models. The complete circle represents all knowledge (omniscience). It is this complete circle (the mind of God) to which the prophets of religion claim at least partial access. If scientists were to accept these claims as working hypotheses, then perhaps such acceptance would bring them that much closer to the infinite circle that they could never otherwise hope to reach.

This proposition raises a number of questions, however. For example: How much of the divine mind can we gain access to through religion? How much of religion can scientists reasonably be expected to incorporate into any new scientific–religious theories? Which religions, and which aspects of those religions, conform most with rationality? Which aspects of both science and religion are 'right' or 'best'? If we can answer these questions, then perhaps we will have the makings of a scientific–religious synthesis (a bird that uses both wings to fly!).

Anjam Khursheed suggests that two principles may be applied to help us in 'the sifting of essential religious truth from man-made religious fallacy'. The first of these is an independent investigation of the truth (independent from religious dogma or prejudice), with acceptance of only that which conforms to reason and science. He argues that

> while religious truth must ultimately be taken on faith, this faith need not be blind. Although there are many religious beliefs that cannot be tested in the traditional manner in which scientific hypotheses

related to the material world are tested and observed, yet it should not be assumed that we are therefore obliged to abandon our rational faculty when dealing with such issues . . . Weighing religious doctrines and tenets 'in the balance of reason and science' can enable us to distinguish the pure or essential elements of a religion from erroneous traditions and man-made dogmas.[28]

The second principle is to ask what the *fruits* of any given religion or religious belief may be. This investigation should not be based on the behaviour of a religion's professed adherents, as this may have gone wildly astray from its founder's original teachings. It is rather the life of the founder and the quality of his teachings that should be investigated and assessed. This principle argues that even if we cannot prove something scientifically, provided it does not conflict with reason (based on the first principle), we should accept it if it produces socially desirable results. This is summarized by Khursheed as follows:

All the major religions known to man stress spiritual principles such as the importance of love, truthfulness, concern for others etc. Such principles are not empirically testable in any scientific sense. However, it may be argued that if belief in an unempirical notion puts mankind on a path to social progress and unity, or assists us to better understand ourselves or the world, it must be right to so believe.[29]

Khursheed also points out that religion cannot be faulted for employing 'empirically untestable generalities', which science itself uses (faith in the existence of universal laws which cannot be tested, for example). Ultimately, the validity of science can only be assessed by examining its fruits. This would, therefore, seem to be a reasonable principle to adopt when testing the validity of a given religion or religious belief.

These two principles thus provide a rational basis for making sense of the variety of religious tenets that we must consider. Further clarification may be obtained from the Bahá'í view of the role of religion.

According to this view, God has left us free to choose between the two sides of our nature: the lower self, which is associated with physical 'animal' needs, and the higher self, the distinguishing characteristic of humanity, which enables us to think and feel independently of our own immediate desires. 'Self-fulfilment' is attained through the cultivation of this higher self. If the lower self acquires a position of dominance then the individual will sink far below his or her potential. Despite this freedom to choose, however, we need some external assistance to show us our unsuspected potentialities. The normal sources of knowledge, empirical investigation and rational deduction and induction, are inadequate. The required inspiration and imagination come at certain critical points in history from the religious prophets or 'manifestations of God', who have perspective and extraordinary insight into the meaning of life. These divine educators are the founders of the great religions, of whom Abraham, Moses, Buddha, Zoroaster, Jesus, Muhammad and Bahá'u'lláh are examples.[30]

This is what religion has to offer science – the insights into the meaning of life that the prophets claim to have received direct from God. Irrespective of the source of this inspiration, science must ask whether or not it conforms to reason and whether or not it produces any human benefit. If any of the prophets' teachings meet these two standards, then science should seek ways of including them in a new scientific–religious synthesis. Similarly, religion might benefit from a reconsideration of the importance of any teachings or practices that do not meet these standards.

Science and religion should find unity in their mutual quest for universal truth. No matter which road we take, the search for ultimate answers always leads to the infinite. Is there really any difference between the infinite encountered by scientists (in concepts such as 'black holes', quantum 'waves', or the big bang 'singularity') and the Infinite (or God) of religion? As Paul Davies points out:

> In our quest for ultimate answers it is hard not to be drawn, in one way or another, to the infinite. Whether it is an infinite tower of turtles, an infinity of parallel worlds, an infinite set of mathematical propositions, or an infinite Creator, physical existence surely cannot be rooted in anything finite.[31]

MANY RELIGIONS, ONE TRUTH

One of the central ideas of the Bahá'í Faith is that of progressive revelation. The Absolute Truth is infinitely beyond the present range of human understanding, and our conceptions of it must develop gradually, according to this view, through God's revelation and guidance. Our earlier, imperfect ideas are replaced, as time goes on, by more and more adequate conceptions as revealed by God, according to our capacity.

Bahá'u'lláh claims that all true religions come from the same divine source, that all the prophets of God proclaim the Word of God, and that religious truth is continuous and relative, not final and absolute. This message is conveyed clearly in the following teaching, taken from the Bahá'í writings:

> Know thou assuredly that the essence of all the Prophets is one and the same. Their unity is absolute.

God, the Creator saith: There is no distinction what-soever among the Bearers of My Message. They all have but one purpose; their secret is the same secret. It is clear and evident, therefore, that any apparent variation in the intensity of their light is not inherent in the light itself, but rather should be attributed to the varying receptivity of an ever-changing world. Every Prophet Whom the Almighty and Peerless Creator hath purposed to send to the peoples of the earth hath been entrusted with a Message, and charged to act in a manner that would best meet the requirements of the age in which he appeared.[32]

Two aspects to the teachings of the prophets or educators are distinguished. Firstly, they all have in common the same universal themes concerning our attitude towards God, our fellow human beings, and the universe: love, justice, detach-ment from personal desire, honesty, selflessness, faithfulness, humility, forgiveness, charity, obedience, mercy, trustworthi-ness, sincerity, truthfulness, moderation, and so on. Secondly, each includes social teachings or practical guide-lines relevant to the contemporary level of development and needs of the society.[33] In the final analysis, however, they are all 'lamps lit from the same Light'.[34]

The idea of progressive revelation also comes across in the teachings of Jesus to his disciples:

I have yet many things to say unto you, but ye cannot bear them now. Howbeit when he, the Spirit of truth is come, he will guide you into all truth: for he shall not speak of himself; but whatsoever he shall hear, that shall he speak: and he will shew you all things to come.

(John 16, 12–13)

Progressive revelation is a concept that can enable the scientist to make sense of the many different religions. It provides a framework for integration between different religions (by taking account of the teachings of all the great prophets) and between science and religion (through its evolutionary perspective).

Religious writer M.K. Rohani brings this point out in a recent book entitled *Accents of God*.[35] Rohani examines six of the world's major religions – Hinduism, Judaism, Buddhism, Christianity, Islam, and the Bahá'í Faith – and concludes that:

> Each of these religious traditions has its own distinctive form of expression that reflects its cultural and historical setting. Nevertheless, they all hold in common certain essential teachings with regard to the nature, meaning and purpose of life. Primarily, there are three themes intrinsic to each of these great religions. First, they all teach that there is an eternal changeless reality that transcends the temporal and limited world of everyday existence. Second, each asserts that this eternal reality is within the grasp of us all – all human beings can acquire the eternal and divine attributes of love, patience, detachment, forgiveness and so on, and thereby attain to a peace that enables us to overcome the difficulties of this life. Third, they all affirm that the attainment of this reality is both the purpose of our existence and the way to true happiness. All religions have expounded on these basic principles in some form and have provided a way to achieve this ultimate and eternal goal.[36]

There are many religions in the world today. Christianity is the largest, embracing over one-fifth of the world's population,[37] followed by Islam, Hinduism, Buddhism, Confucianism,

Shinto, Taoism, Judaism (in that order) and a wide range of others. Within these broad groupings, there are, of course, numerous sects and denominations. The six major religions examined by Rohani are, however, the most widespread and therefore warrant at least some attempt at an overview.

i) Hinduism

Hinduism has the third largest religious following in the world. It is polytheistic (although the numerous gods and goddesses now tend to be viewed as manifestations of a single divine essence, *Brahman*), and is based principally in India, parts of Pakistan, Bangladesh, Sri Lanka, Nepal and Sikkim. Having no single founder, it evolved largely from Vedism, the religion of the ancient Indo-Europeans who settled in India during the second millennium BC.

A Hindu can best be described as one who bases his or her beliefs and way of life on 'the complex system of faith and practice which has grown up organically in the Indian sub-continent over a period of at least three millennia'.[38] Hinduism is both a civilization and a conglomerate of religions, without any central authority or organization. Some argue that many of its sects are so different that it should no longer be regarded as a single religion.[39]

In principle, Hinduism incorporates all forms of belief (including atheism). All religions are declared to be appropriate ways to the one divine goal. The Hindu is inclined to revere the divine in every manifestation, and is therefore tolerant of other doctrines, to the extent that it is possible for a Hindu to embrace a non-Hindu religion without ceasing to be a Hindu. All religions are regarded as complementary aspects of the same ultimate truth.

By analogy, if you leave four blind men alone in a room with an elephant, and later ask them to describe the elephant on the basis of the parts that they encountered, you may receive four different descriptions, all true. But it is still a single elephant. This is the doctrine of syncretism, which accepts all religions as true (inadequate, perhaps, but true nonetheless).

In addition to its syncretic nature, the other most out-standing and common characteristic of Hinduism is monism (a philosophy claiming that everything is ultimately One). The many gods and goddesses contained in the Vedas (the original Hindu scriptures) were a problem, but the Upanishads (later scriptures) reduced them from 3,306 to thirty-three, to three, and finally to a single divine essence.[40] This one reality that underlies everything in the universe, manifesting itself in a multitude of forms, is called *Brahman*. It is infinite, beyond our comprehension, the 'soul' and creator of all things.

Our perception of a fragmented world, in which we can act independently from our environment, is merely an illusion (*maya*). Humanity's attachment to worldly objects, and its failure to see beyond the illusion of *maya* to the reality of *Brahman*, means that it remains bound by *karma* (a series of rebirths, the nature of each being determined by one's deeds). Until we attain liberation from the world, we remain trapped in an unending stream of periodic returns to life under the law of *karma* ('As a man sows, so shall he reap'). The misfortunes of life are seen to be self-inflicted – the result of bad *karma*. There are essentially three ways to break the cycle, and thus attain liberation[41]:

1) 'The path of duties' (*karma-marga*) – disinterested discharge of ritual and social obligations;

2) 'The path of knowledge' (*jnanamarga*) – use of medita-tion (*yoga*) to gain a supra-intellectual insight into one's identity with *Brahman*.

3) 'The path of devotion' (*bhakti-marga*) – devotion to a personal God.

Each of these ways is deemed suitable for different types of people. For the ordinary Hindu, the first path will be the natural one to choose. Conformity to social and ritual duties ensures that the fundamental equilibrium of the cosmos, nature and society is not upset.

As many of the new age thinkers, such as Fritjof Capra and Gary Zukav, have demonstrated, this religion has parallels with some of the findings of modern physics.[42] All things are seen as interdependent and inseparable parts of an organic and ever-changing cosmic whole. All phenomena in the world are viewed as manifestations of an underlying unity. These ideas are consistent with the latest scientific thinking. The essence of Hinduism cannot, therefore, be seen as conflicting with science, and one would certainly expect some human benefits from its social teachings.

ii) Judaism

Judaism is the oldest of the West's major religions, and is the root from which Christianity, Islam and the Bahá'í Faith have grown.[43] Its cornerstone is the Pentateuch or Five Books of Moses contained in the Old Testament of the Bible (Genesis, Exodus, Leviticus, Numbers, and Deuteronomy). The Pentateuch (also known as the Law or Torah) is considered to be the direct and most fundamental revelation as delivered to Moses on Mount Sinai.[44]

Moses is regarded by some as the founder of Judaism.[45] In other sources, Abraham is taken to be its founder.[46] In any case, the God of Israel is identified as the creator of the world, who entered into a covenant with Abraham (*circa* 1900 BC). God's promises to Abraham were fulfilled through Moses, who led the Exodus from Egypt, imposed further obligations on Israel at Mount Sinai, and brought his people to Canaan (*circa* 1250–1210 BC).

The fundamental obligations imposed by Moses were the Ten Commandments, as revealed to him by God. The first of these had an important part to play in the introduction of monotheism and a movement away from idolatry. The remaining Commandments provided a guide for moral behaviour and may be viewed as God's first major step in His plan to guide humanity from a self-centred embryonic state to that of a selfless maturity, in which all behaviour is directed towards the benefit of the whole.

We are all seen as being in a covenant relationship with God, a relationship that Jews develop by example and witness. Humanity has a dual nature capable of both obedience and disobedience to God's law and, within this context, exercises ethical freedom in making choices between good and evil impulses. Sin is the deliberate disobedience of the Law or Torah.

Most Jews still await the arrival of the Messiah ('anointed'), who will bring knowledge of God and establish His Kingdom on the earth. Christians, of course, believe that the Messiah has already appeared in Jesus, while Muslims believe that God sent a further (and final) Messenger in Muhammad.

Since the Holocaust of World War II, Judaism has become a non-European religion centred in Israel, with substantial numbers of adherents in Russia and the United States. Within each of these communities it is being faced with increasing secularization.

As with Hinduism, there is nothing contained in the heart of Judaism which is in conflict with science. The idea of a single God or source of creation is consistent with the indivisible quantum reality of physics. If we take the act of creation to be an ongoing process which God is continuously engaged in (as opposed to the 'watchmaker' notion of creation), then the underlying unity discovered by physicists may be taken as evidence of the existence of such a God.[47]

The guidelines on behaviour contained in the Pentateuch, while possibly in need of some updating (see particularly Leviticus 18–20), must generally be viewed as beneficial to human welfare. The commandments to 'love the Lord thy God with all thine heart' (Deuteronomy 6.5) and to 'love thy neighbour as thyself' (Leviticus 19.18) were later taken by Jesus to be the most important, and these now form the basis of Christianity.

iii) Buddhism

Siddhartha Gautama, born around 560 BC, was the man who became the Buddha, the fully Enlightened One. He was born of a royal family of the Sakya clan in Kapilavastu on the borders of Nepal and India. At the age of twenty-nine, after an early life of luxury and ease, he underwent a dramatic change.

Siddhartha became deeply aware, as if for the first time, that all beings were subject to aging, sickness and death. He saw the truth of change and the impermanence of things. The realization hit him with such force that his luxurious lifestyle completely lost its appeal. He suddenly wanted to know the reasons for life's woes – why people suffered in poverty and sickness; why all creatures were born, apparently just to die. In search of truth and enlightenment, he left home (leaving his wife and child behind), and lived as other holy men in India, wearing rags and begging food. He learned self-discipline, how to meditate, and how to perform rites and rituals.

After six years of searching, which left him weak and close to death, Siddhartha realized the futility of his actions. He suddenly understood that killing the senses, through religious rites and rituals, was as bad as over-indulging the senses. Whilst resting under a tree, he touched the earth with his hand, and called upon it to bear witness, saying he would not move from that spot until he received enlightenment. His mind suddenly became tranquil, yet alert. He observed the nature of existence, the nature of desire; he observed that dissatisfaction and suffering arose when desire arose. He experienced the total cessation of desire and realized that this was the cessation of all suffering – he became the Fully Awakened One, Buddha.[48]

For the following forty-five years the Buddha taught devotees and disciples of all kinds. At the heart of his teachings lay the Four Noble Truths. First, it is asserted that existence is full of conflict, dissatisfaction, sorrow, and suffering. Second, this is seen to be caused by selfish desire. Third, liberation from this suffering (*Nirvana*) is viewed as attainable. Fourth, the Noble Eightfold Path is regarded as the way to liberation. The Noble Eightfold Path, or 'middle way', involves striving for rightness in eight areas of life: view, thought, speech, action, mode of living, endeavour, mindfulness, and concentration.

The Hindu concepts of *maya* and *karma* are also present in Buddhist philosophy. Belief in an independent self and attachment to worldly possessions is regarded as a delusion by Buddhists as it is by most Hindus, and one's deeds are seen to contribute to the harvest that one reaps in this life or in the next. The continuous stream of rebirths is once again a feature of this religion. Enlightenment or liberation is sought through ridding oneself of the delusion of ego. This is achieved by following the Eightfold Path.

Like Hinduism, Buddhism has parallels with modern physics, with concepts such as impermanence and interdependence.[49] Self-denial and service to the community are also central aspects of this religion.

iv) Christianity

I don't think it matters who Christ was as long as one tries to imitate him in his noble life and self-denial.
— *F. York Powell* in a letter to E.G. Punchard[50]

There are a great many Christian writers who have tackled the question of who Jesus was and what his message was for humanity. Perhaps the best known and most highly esteemed of these was C.S. Lewis, who was an atheist for many years until he became 'the most dejected and reluctant convert in all England'. Walter Hooper speaks of Lewis's conversion as an 'experience that helped him to understand not only apathy but active unwillingness to accept religion'.[51] He goes on to say that, 'as a Christian writer, gifted with an exceptionally brilliant and logical mind and a lucid, lively style, he [Lewis] was without peer'.

Lewis, in his analysis of Christ, concludes that there is general agreement (even among 'anti-God' people) that in the teachings of Jesus and his followers, moral truth is exhibited at its purest and best. 'It is not sloppy idealism, it is full of wisdom and shrewdness'.[52]

The difficulty for many lies not in the moral teachings of Jesus, but in some of the claims he made about himself. C.S. Lewis sums up the issue most succinctly.

'What are we to make of Christ?' There is no question of what we can make of Him, it is entirely a question of what He intends to make of us. You must accept or reject the story.

The things He says are very different from what any other teacher has said. Others say, 'This is the truth about the universe. This is the way you ought to go,' but He says, 'I am the Truth, and the Way, and the Life.' He says, 'No man can reach absolute reality, except through Me. Try to retain your own life and you will be inevitably ruined. Give yourself away and you will be saved.' He says, 'If you are ashamed of Me, if, when you hear this call, you turn the other way, I also will look the other way when I come again as

God without disguise. If anything whatever is keeping you from God and from Me, whatever it is, throw it away. If it is your eye, pull it out. If it is your hand, cut it off. If you put yourself first you will be last. Come to me everyone who is carrying a heavy load, I will set that right. Your sins, all of them, are wiped out, I can do that. I am Re-birth, I am Life. Eat Me, drink Me, I am your Food. And finally, do not be afraid, I have overcome the whole Universe.' That is the issue.[53]

When the word 'I' is interpreted in the mystical sense to mean God, then these claims begin to make sense ('I and my Father are one' – John 10.30). You are left with the choice – Jesus was either a mystic (who had attained unity with God by giving up all attachment to the personal self), or a prophet (chosen by God as a messenger), or he was God incarnate (as most Christians claim). Does it really matter whether God spoke directly to us in Jesus, or whether He spoke to us indirectly *through* Jesus ('Believe me that I am in the Father, and the Father in me: or else believe me for the very works' sake' – John 14.11)? Neither the moral teachings of Christ, nor his controversial claims seem, to me, to be in any way incompatible with either science or wisdom.

Many self-improvement books are filled with evidence of the power of Christ and the enormous personal benefit that can be gained by following his guidance. Al Koran refers to him as 'The Great Psychologist'[54]; Norman Vincent Peale bases his whole philosophy on his teachings[55]; and Clement Stone points to the Bible as the greatest self-help book ever written.[56]

If we forget about the trimmings added by different religious groups on the basis of their varying, and often conflicting, interpretations of different parts of the Bible, then we find that Jesus was simply asking us to give up our attachment to the self (including our selfish desires, our assumed possessions, and our belief in self-sufficiency) and to believe instead in God. The doctrine of love (for God and our fellow human beings) was therefore central to his message.

> And one of the scribes came, and having heard them reasoning together, and perceiving that he had answered them well, asked him, Which is the first commandment of all?
>
> And Jesus answered him, The first of all the commandments is, Hear, O Israel; The Lord our God is one Lord:
>
> And thou shalt love the Lord thy God with all thy heart, and with all thy soul, and with all thy mind, and with all thy strength: this is the first commandment.
>
> And the second is like, namely this, Thou shalt love thy neighbour as thyself. There is none other commandment greater than these.
>
> (Mark 12.28–31)

Love, it has been said, means many things to many people. For me, it is a motivator – not just any motivator, but the greatest of all motivators. Whatever your personal definition of love, would you not sacrifice anything for the one person or thing that you would claim to love most? Would you say that you feel a great attraction or desire to be near your most loved one? Would you describe this attraction as more than physical? Would you agree that this experience involves a desire to please the one you love? Would it be fair to say that your love would be complete if the two of you lived in total harmony as one being? Does your love not involve a desire for unity; for togetherness; for integration; for shared experience; for a common existence? Does your love not seem something like that 'groping for integrity' referred to by Birch, in his view of the purpose of life[57]? Is that not what life is really all about – to love and to be loved? Is it not from love that we obtain a sense of purpose or meaning? Without love, what would we have?

When Jesus tells us to love our neighbour, he wants us to do more than just behave in a manner that pleases our neighbour. He wants us to transcend the bounds of selfish desire; to fill our hearts with the power of selflessness; to benefit mutually from a genuine desire to help one another; to not only act for the good of all, but to feel for all around you; to express passion and concern for the world around you, and to experience the passion and concern that it will give back to you in return.

In the words of the Apostle, Paul: 'whatsoever a man soweth, that shall he also reap' (Galatians 5.7). Love the world, and it will love you back. Hate the world, and you will be consumed by your own hate. The harvest that you reap in this world will be determined by the seeds that you sow. That, I believe, is why caring people generally tend to be happier than those who are more concerned with themselves.

The words of the philosopher, Ecclesiastes (quoted on pp. 30–31) highlight this point. A man with everything ultimately had nothing, because he had no love for others or for anything outside himself. This is what Jesus warned us about when he posed the question:

> For what shall it profit a man, if he shall gain the whole world, and lose his own soul?
>
> (Mark 8.36)

The road to love is not easy, however. We may find it easy to love a chosen few in our lives (a common phenomenon that may be construed as a mere extension of egotism).[58] But how can we love everyone? How can you 'love your enemies', as Jesus asked of us? How can you love a man who has just raped your daughter, or one who has just killed your son?

If everyone in the world were to follow the advice of Jesus, then such a dilemma would not, of course, arise. But until the world has matured sufficiently to accept such advice, we are clearly left with a problem. Until the time comes when the word 'enemy' becomes obsolete, we must try harder to include these people in our love. We must follow the example of Gordon Wilson, who moved many people to tears, through his compassion in the face of tremendous grief. He had just lost his daughter in the Enniskillen massacre, yet he was able to forgive the people responsible for planting the bomb that killed her. For a few minutes, while he related his story and his forgiveness on television, Catholics and Protestants of Northern Ireland were united. Such is the power of love.

Jesus said that the second commandment was like the first. We must love God and our neighbour. Indeed, it seems that it is not possible to love God without also loving His people. We are all brothers and sisters; all children of the one God. Whatever you do and feel for others, so shall you do and feel for God.

'I was hungry and you fed me, thirsty and you gave me a drink; I was a stranger and you received me into your homes, naked and you clothed me; I was sick and you took care of me, in prison and you visited me.'

The righteous will then answer him, 'When, Lord, did we ever see you hungry and feed you, or thirsty and give you a drink? When did we ever see you a stranger and welcome you in our homes, or naked and clothe you? When did we ever see you sick or in prison, and visit you?'

The King will reply, 'I tell you, whenever you did this for one of the least important of these brothers of mine, you did it for me!'

Then he will say to those on his left, 'Away from me, you that are under God's curse! . . . I was hungry but you would not feed me, thirsty but you would not give me a drink; I was a stranger but you would not welcome me in your homes, naked but you would not clothe me; I was sick and in prison but you would not take care of me.'

Then they will answer him, 'When, Lord, did we ever see you hungry or thirsty or a stranger or naked or sick or in prison, and we would not help you?'

The King will reply, 'I tell you, whenever you refused to help one of these least important ones, you refused to help me.'

(Matthew 25.31–45)

We must deny ourselves, put ourselves last, die to the self daily, and be 'born again' to a love and faith that transcends the bounds of self. For only in this way can we save ourselves.

If any man will come after me, let him deny himself, and take up his cross daily, and follow me. For whosoever will save his life will lose it: but whosoever will lose his life for my sake, the same shall save it.

(Luke 9.23–24)

Nothing that Jesus is reported to have said can be found to conflict with reason or to bear anything other than 'good fruit' for his most faithful followers. Although he spoke mostly in parables to make it easier for the people of the time to understand, thus leaving much open to interpretation, the underlying theme of love and self-denial is nevertheless clear.

v) Islam

The religion of Islam was founded by the prophet Muhammad in the early part of the seventh century AD. Muhammad was born in the small town of Mecca in the mountains of what is now Saudi Arabia. Orphaned by the age of six, he accompanied his uncle on trading caravans that travelled between Mecca and Syria, until, at the age of twenty-five, he married a rich widow who employed him to run her business.

During his commercial career, he became discontented with the traditional tribal religion, which was polytheistic and superstitious, and with the self-centred, grasping economic individualism of the traders of Mecca. At the age of forty he had a religious experience that convinced him of his divine call to be the Apostle of the One and only God, Alláh. In a vision, he saw the archangel Gabriel carrying a piece of silk with the word *Recite* on it. Upon asking, 'What shall I recite?', he received the following reply:

> Recite in the name of your Lord, the Creator,
> Who created man from clots of blood!
> Recite! Your Lord is the Most Bounteous One,
> Who by the pen has taught mankind
> Things they did not know.
>
> (Qur'án 96, 1–4)

This was to be the first of many divine revelations to Muhammad. These revelations continued over a twenty-three year period, and were recorded in the *suras* which constitute the Holy Qur'án. The Qur'án claims to be the greatest spiritual force, which is ultimately destined to bring the whole of humanity to perfection.[59]

Qur'ánic theology is rigorously monotheistic – God is unique, omnipotent, omniscient and merciful. Humanity is exhorted to obey His will (that is, to be Muslim). For the

Muslims, the Qur'án is the Word of God, confirming and consummating earlier revealed books (such as contained in the Christian Bible) and thereby replacing them. The Prophet Muhammad is deemed to be the last and most perfect of a series of messengers of God to humanity – from Adam through Abraham to Moses and Jesus. The Qur'án has great reverence for Jesus, whom it variously refers to as Son of Mary, Messiah, Prophet, Word, Servant and Spirit of God,[60] but it regards him and all other prophets (including Muhammad) as human, thereby denying the Christian Trinity.

Whilst a good deal of the Qur'án is concerned with legislation for marriage, divorce, personal and social relationships (appropriate to the time and place of its inception), its primary message is the unity of God and the condemnation of idolatry ('There is no god but Alláh'). At that time in the Arab world, there were many gods and goddesses, and countless idols. In order to communicate the truth of the divine unity, God has sent His messengers or prophets, who throughout history have been calling us back to Him. Because of our weak nature, we are prone to forget or even wilfully reject the divine unity and our dependence on God. In our pride (the cardinal sin of humanity), we foolishly believe that we are self-sufficient.

The purpose of the existence of humanity is seen as submission to the divine will. Whereas the rest of nature obeys God automatically, humanity alone possesses the choice to obey or disobey. Recognition of the unity of God entails a moral struggle, which necessitates freeing ourselves from narrowness of mind and smallness of heart. We must go beyond ourselves and use our possessions for the sake of others. Hoarding of wealth without recognizing the needs of the poor is declared to be one of the main causes of social decay and one of the greatest sins. This doctrine of social service is an integral part of Islamic teaching, and has contributed to a strong feeling of brotherhood amongst Muslims.

As with the teachings of Jesus, there is great wisdom in the message delivered by Muhammad. Whilst many Christians may not be happy about the denial of the concept of Trinity or the incarnation of Christ, or Muhammad's many wives (after the death of his first wife), or his endorsement of the use of force on occasions, it can be argued that if the teachings are from God then whether or not the prophet is God incarnate is irrelevant, and that polygamy and the use of force were appropriate to the time and place. In any case, Muslims do not claim that Muhammad was God incarnate, but only that he acted as a messenger of God.

Once again, the message of self-denial and service to the whole is evident. The fundamental teachings of Muhammad have clear potential human benefit and in no way conflict with science.

vi) The Bahá'í Faith

There can be no doubt whatever that the peoples of the world, of whatever race or religion, derive their inspiration from one heavenly Source, and are the subjects of one God. The difference between the ordinances under which they abide should be attributed to the varying requirements and exigencies of the age in which they were revealed.

— *Bahá'u'lláh*[61]

Any Religion which is not a cause of love and unity is no religion . . . All the Manifestations of God and His Prophets have taught the same truths and given the same spiritual law. They all teach the one code of morality. There is no division in the truth.

—*'Abdu'l-Bahá*[62]

The Bahá'í Faith is a relatively new religion. It originated in Persia with the teachings of Siyyid 'Alí-Muhammad, the *Báb* (Arabic for 'gate'), who suffered persecution and was martyred in 1850. It is estimated that about 20,000 followers, of what was then known as the Bábí Faith, were slain during this persecution. His successor was Mírzá Husayn-'Alí, who was given the title of Bahá'u'lláh ('The Glory of God'). Bahá'u'lláh died in 1892, after spending the last thirty-nine years of his life in exile and imprisonment for allegedly posing a threat to the Muslim religion in both Persia and the Ottoman Empire. He left a vast accumulation of writings that are now treasured as the sacred scriptures of the Bahá'í Faith.

The Bahá'í Faith is not eclectic or syncretic. It is not an offshoot of Islam, or a sect of any other religion, and it does not claim to receive its inspiration from the sacred books of other religions. Bahá'u'lláh asserts that his message is a revelation direct from God. He and the founders of the world's major religions are regarded as 'Manifestations of God'. Whilst God, in essence, is unknowable, His Word is progressively revealed to us (in accordance with our growing capacity to comprehend) through His chosen Messengers or Prophets, the latest being Bahá'u'lláh. He will, in turn, be followed by others – a point that was difficult for the Muslims of Persia and Turkey to accept, as Muhammad is regarded by Muslims as the final Prophet.

Bahá'í writer David Hofman sums up the concept of progressive revelation as follows:

> The guidance of God is given to man from age to age through His Christs. At one time the Christ is called Jesus, at another Buddha, at others Moses, Muhammad, Krishna, Bahá'u'lláh. *It is always the same Christ.* Just as the sun is called Monday, Tuesday,

Wednesday; or March, April, May or 1960, 1961, 1962; it is always the same sun.[63]

The oneness of God, the oneness of religion, and the oneness of humanity constitute the three basic principles of the Bahá'í Faith.[64] Its main aims are to unite all religions and to unite all people (through a 'unity in diversity' that permits, and even welcomes, differences), and, in doing so, to bring peace to the whole world. Bahá'u'lláh wrote, 'The religion of God is for love and unity; make it not the cause of enmity or dissension'.[65]

Bahá'u'lláh also taught that harmony should exist between science and religion, that men and women should be regarded as equal, that all the people of the world should be educated, and that extremes of wealth and poverty should be eradicated.

The highest ethical and moral behaviour is required of Bahá'ís through the development of such attributes as honesty, cleanliness, courtesy, humility, trustworthiness, justice, compassion, forgiveness, chastity and fidelity. These attributes must govern their daily lives. They must, in addition, serve humanity in whatever way they can as a form of worship to God.[66] 'Abdu'l-Bahá (Bahá'u'lláh's eldest son, who succeeded him as head of the faith after his death) urged followers of the faith to live their lives in accordance with the following standards:

> To be no cause of grief to anyone. To be kind to all people and to love them . . . To be silent concerning the faults of others . . . To look always at the good and not at the bad . . . To sever our hearts from ourselves and from the world. To be humble. To be servants to each other . . . To act with cautiousness and wisdom. To be truthful. To be hospitable. To be

reverent. To be a cause of healing for every sick one, a comforter for every sorrowful one, a pleasant water for every thirsty one, a heavenly table for every hungry one, a star to every horizon, a light for every lamp, a herald to everyone who yearns for the kingdom of God.[67]

The Bahá'í Faith, through its encouragement of an independent search for truth (independent of religious dogma and prejudice) and its emphasis on the complementary nature of science and religion, serves to provide a framework for scientific and religious synthesis. In urging us to examine the teachings of the great religious founders at their source without prejudice, and regarding them all as aspects of the same truth, it also provides a potential framework for the synthesis of all major religions. When viewed in the context of progressive revelation, they begin to make much more sense. They all conform to the two principles that Khursheed suggests we test them against[68] – their fundamental teachings conform with reason and science, and they also yield 'good fruit'. It is only the superstition and small-mindedness of some of their 'followers' that leads them into conflict with science and with each other.

The famous historian Arnold Toynbee also concludes (on the basis of historical studies of Hinduism, Judaism, Buddhism, Christianity, Islam, and Zoroastrianism) that all religions have a common essence.[69] He identifies religion with an experience of a 'spiritual presence' or Absolute Reality, which cannot be comprehended by the human mind. Humanity seeks to be in harmony with this presence, because it contains both the meaning of life and the good for which we thirst. The message that he gleans from all the religions of his studies is that harmony with the Absolute Reality can only be attained through the relinquishment of self-centredness.

The imperative of thinking or caring for others is common to all the major religions. There is one very clear message, one truth – happiness and harmony can only be attained through selflessness. In other words, you can serve the self best by renouncing your attachment to it. Do what you do in the service of God (that is, the Absolute Reality, the underlying unity, or the source of creation) and not in the service of self.

The predominant message from Hinduism is one of self-denial, with the self and everything else that we perceive in this world regarded as mere illusion; reality lies only in the divine essence or underlying unity. Moses tells us that we should put God or the source of creation before all else, and that we should not put ourselves before others. The Buddha informs us that liberation from suffering can only be attained by giving up all selfish desires. Jesus says that we should love God and one another, and that whoever puts himself first will be last. Muhammad emphasizes the divine unity and our dependence on God; we must submit to the divine will, go beyond ourselves, and use our possessions for the sake of others. Bahá'u'lláh speaks of the 'prison of self' and informs us that our purpose is to know and love God and to grow towards Him.

The one truth is, therefore, this – liberation from suffering, or the attainment of enlightenment, or heaven, or nirvana, or the kingdom of God (or whatever term may be applied to it) may only be achieved by giving up attachment to the self (giving up self consciousness in exchange for God consciousness).

The great prophet of science, Albert Einstein, had something similar to say about the self.

The true value of a human being is determined primarily by the measure and the sense in which he has attained liberation from the self.[70]

Whether or not you believe in a God, there is, as physicist Paul Davies puts it, 'powerful evidence that there is "something going on" behind it all'.[71] Even if the impression of order or design in the universe does not convince you that there is an intelligence or a purpose above the level of humanity, there is still no reason to ignore completely the extraordinary human wisdom contained within the teachings of the world's major religions.

When all the superfluous dogma and ritual is stripped away, we find that they all convey the same fundamental message – the need for humanity to recognize and serve an underlying unity, and the need for self-denial in the path of spiritual progress. None of this is in conflict with science.

So how, then, should we act upon this message? How can we free ourselves from the prison of self and grow towards God, the supreme being or underlying unity of all things? How can we integrate this notion into a new scientific-religious synthesis? The answer, I believe, lies in mysticism – a key aspect of all religions, and an area that is attracting increasing attention from scientists.

MYSTICAL
CONSCIOUSNESS

Mysticism is particularly prominent in the eastern
religions of Hinduism, Buddhism and Taoism, but I
would argue that it lies at the heart of all religions, and is, in
fact, the common essence of religion. Mysticism also forms
the basis, I believe, for the latest scientific thinking. For this
reason, it provides an important link between science and
religion, as Capra and others have convincingly argued.[1]

In this chapter, I will attempt to develop this link by
drawing out the relationship between science, religion and
mysticism. In doing so, I hope to bring together some of the
themes presented in earlier chapters.

MYSTICISM AND RELIGION

Mysticism has been defined as 'the apprehension of an
ultimate nonsensuous unity in all things'.[2] The mystical experience involves 'an extension of normal consciousness, a release
of latent powers and a widening of vision, so that aspects of
truth unplumbed by the rational intellect are revealed'.[3]

For those who believe in the existence of God, the
mystical experience involves an awareness of the presence of

God. In believers and non-believers alike, it evokes an awareness of being part of something (a cosmic whole) that is much greater than the self. This increased awareness may be called 'cosmic consciousness' or 'God consciousness'. The mystic believes that he or she is in communion either with a personal 'God' or with some impersonal 'Ultimate Reality'. F.C. Happold, in his book *Mysticism*, identifies seven marked characteristics of the mystical state.[4]

First, it defies expression in terms that can be readily understood by one who has never experienced it. As it involves a higher level of consciousness, it is difficult to communicate the experience in terms of the lower level. Secondly, it results in insights that would not be available at the level of ordinary consciousness. A depth of knowledge is acquired, and even though the person undergoing the experience may not be able to express this knowledge in 'the language of the intellect', she is convinced with absolute certainty of her newly found wisdom. Thirdly, the mystical state is transient. It rarely lasts for a long time, although it is possible to increase the frequency of mystical experiences by following a certain way of life. Fourthly, it involves passivity. While it is possible to prepare oneself for the reception of mystical experience (through meditative techniques, for example[5]), it is not possible to induce it at will. A fifth common characteristic is a consciousness of unity. All feelings of duality and multiplicity are obliterated, including the distinction between the self and the rest of the universe, and even the distinction between self and deity. Sixthly, there is a sense of timelessness. Distinctions between time and space disappear (as in Einstein's four-dimensional universe). Finally, the mystical experience leaves one with the conviction that the ego, or self, that we are normally familiar with, is not the real 'I'. There is another self, a true self that is immortal, unchanging, and not bound by space–time (the *Atman* of Hinduism[6] or the *Universal Self* of Jung[7]).

Note the parallels between descriptions of mysticism and Toynbee's description of the common essence of all religions. The Absolute Reality taught by religion is ultimately mysterious; it is the fount of all knowledge; it is the unity that underlies all things in the universe; and harmony with it may only be attained through self-sacrifice.[8]

A common essence is shared by mysticism and religion despite their use of different language ('Universal Self' replacing 'God', for example). Also, there seems to be a marked similarity in the ideas of both mystics and prophets about the way to attain harmony with the Ultimate Being or soul of the universe.

The road to mystical or God consciousness (whereby one attains communion with God or harmony with the Absolute Reality) is referred to by F.C. Happold as the 'Mystic Way'. He describes it as follows:

> It is the Way of Union through reciprocal love, of like calling unto like, of the love of God stretching down to man and of the love of man stretching up to God. But it is not an easy way. It is the Royal Road of the Holy Cross, a way of utter self-loss, of the shedding of every vestige of self-love, of the abandonment of everything, even of one's own selfhood.[9]

There are three stages along this way. Firstly, there is the *Way of Purgation*, involving detachment from the 'things of sense' and 'the death of the egocentric life, so that the divine life may be born in the soul and the union with the Godhead attained'.[10] Once the self has been purged, the individual is ready for the next stage, which is the *Way of Illumination*. This is the beginning of mystical consciousness, and involves a transformation of the 'soul' (or essence of the individual), which is illuminated by the 'light of a new reality'. One's perceptions at this point are changed completely. The third and final stage is, presumably, the perfect mystical consciousness experienced by the prophets. Happold refers to this as the *Way of Union*. This is where one enters into the 'kingdom of heaven' or attains 'nirvana' or 'union with the Godhead'. Whatever one wants to call it, we are assured that it is something to be desired. But before we get there we must die to the self. When the self has died, we can be 'born again' into a spiritual life infinitely beyond our present materialistic existence.

The Christian mystic Joel S. Goldsmith talks in terms of a 'spiritual path' towards 'God-realization'. Once again, the message is one of self-surrender:

> We must surrender all desire to the *one* desire: to see God face to face, to know Him, and to let the will of God be made manifest in us. There must come the complete surrender of our personal selfhood, so that the Spirit of God can fulfill Itself in us in accordance with *Its* will, not with ours . . . We cannot add the kingdom of heaven to our personal sense of self; we cannot attain the kingdom of heaven if there is an inordinate love of personal power, a love of glory, a love of name or fame, or a desire merely to show forth the benefits and the fruitage of the Spirit in the form of better human circumstances. Our vessel must be empty of self before it can be filled with the grace of God.[11]

Bahá'u'lláh uses the analogy of a journey through seven valleys to describe the mystical path or road to God.[12] The journey begins in the *Valley of Search* and continues through those of *Love, Knowledge, Unity, Contentment* and *Wonderment*, until finally the seeker reaches the *Valley of True Poverty and Absolute Nothingness*. Entry into this last valley involves 'the dying from self and the living in God'.[13]

'Abdu'l-Bahá gives this explanation of how we can progress along the path towards God, the mystic's goal:

> Nearness to God is possible through devotion to Him, through entrance into the Kingdom and service to humanity; it is attained by unity with mankind and through loving-kindness to all; it is dependent upon investigation of truth, acquisition of praise-worthy virtues, service in the cause of universal peace and personal sanctification. In a word, nearness to God necessitates sacrifice of self, severance and the giving up of all to Him. Nearness is likeness.[14]

As it says in the Old Testament, 'Let us make man in our image and likeness'.[15] And this is the message common to all religions, that human beings have a divine nature that must be consciously developed. To become our true selves, our fullest selves, we must overcome our attachment to the self and to the material world in which we live. In other words, we must give up the self in order to fulfil the self. Complete elimination of the ego or self would imply a state of absolute perfection, which few could hope to attain, but the mystic way, or path of spiritual progress, requires the subordination of our self and the subjugation of our will to God's, so that we may follow in His way, acquire spiritual qualities and, as far as we can, become *like* God. This is the journey from the hell of conflict, suffering and self to the heaven of peace, happiness and communion with God.

Religion is effectively teaching us the 'mystic way' – the replacement of self-centredness with God-centredness –

although the essence of this teaching has too often been clouded by dogma.

The relationship between religion and mysticism is summarized by Happold as follows:

> The dogmas of religion are the translations into the terms of the intellect, or into evocative symbols, or into a combination of both, of insights which have their origin in mystical intuition . . . Dogmatic statements, especially in so far as they are translations into intellectual concepts, are of necessity translations into the concepts of the age in which they were framed.[16]

Mysticism is communion with the source of all creation, all knowledge and all power – the Absolute Reality, God. In its most perfect form, experienced only by the prophets, mysticism involves union with God (Jesus said, for example, 'I and my father are one'). Through their perfect union with God, their example and their teachings, we receive divine wisdom – the Word of God. While few are chosen for the exalted station of prophethood, many people throughout history have experienced some degree of mystical consciousness, or communion with God.

THE PERENNIAL PHILOSOPHY

Mysticism has been described as the 'perennial philosophy'.[17] It appears to be something that has been with us since the beginning of human consciousness. While ever present in religion (even primitive religion[18]), mystical thinking has continued to manifest itself in various forms in philosophy and science.

The early Greek philosophers retained some sense of the unity of all things, and regarded nature as both universe and pluriverse. Such a position is clearly outlined in Plato's *Laws*:

The ruler of the universe has ordered all things with a view to the excellence and preservation of the whole, and each part, as far as may be, has an action and passion appropriate to it . . . one of these portions of the universe is thine own, unhappy man, which, however little, contributes to the whole; and you do not seem to be aware that this and every other creation is for the sake of the whole, and in order that the life of the whole be blessed; and that you are created for the sake of the whole, and not the whole for the sake of you.[19]

In what is regarded as his greatest work, the *Republic*, Plato uses the analogy of prisoners chained in a cave to describe our position in the physical world in relation to that of the divine reality.[20] From the light of a fire outside, the prisoners view the movement of people outside the cave in the form of shadows cast upon the walls. They can only see things as they really are if they emerge from the cave into the light of the sun. The things we see in the physical world are likened to these shadows, with the realm of truth and reality lying beyond this world.

Aristotle, although differing widely from Plato in many aspects of his philosophy, also believed in the unity of all things. Through our intuitive intelligence (or *nous*), the divine essence contained within each of us, we are, according to Aristotle, able to grasp this unity.[21]

The Stoic philosophers of ancient Greece and Rome promoted a humanist doctrine in the post-Aristotelian period. Stoic moral theory was based on the view that the world, as one great city, is a unity. We, as citizens of the world, have an obligation and loyalty to all things in that city.[22] Epictetus (*circa* AD 60–138) and Marcus Aurelius (AD 121–180), in particular, took this concept of unity furthest.

Epictetus saw all things (both heavenly and earthly) as being united in One. Plants, our bodies, the sun, and everything else in the universe are all viewed as parts of God. There is therefore no distinction drawn between God and the universe. Everything is One – a doctrine that was later to be called Pantheism. The same theme comes across recurrently in the profound and insightful writings contained in *The Meditations of Marcus Aurelius*.

> Constantly regard the universe as one living being, having one substance and one soul; and observe how all things have reference to one perception, the perception of this one living being; and how all things act with one movement; and how all things are the co-operating causes of all things which exist; observe too the continuous spinning of the thread and the contexture of the web . . . And inasmuch as I am in a manner intimately related to the parts which are of the same kind with myself, I shall do nothing unsocial, but I shall rather direct myself to the things which are of the same kind with myself, and I shall turn all my efforts to the common interest, and divert them from the contrary.[23]

Elements of mysticism can also be found in the philosophy of Plotinus (205–270), who talks of a higher power present in all things as 'One Life', and of all living things being made as parts 'with a view to the whole'.

Mysticism appears to have been particularly prevalent in Europe around the end of the Middle Ages and during the Renaissance. The backgrounds and philosophies of some of the most influential mystics of the times are outlined in some detail by Steiner.[24] The most famous of these is probably the German mystic, Meister Eckhart (*circa* 1260–1328), whose teachings contributed to the future development of Protestantism, Romanticism, Idealism, and Existentialism.[25]

The concept of an all-embracing unity has perhaps been developed most fully in the pantheistic doctrine of the Jewish rationalist, Benedict Spinoza (1632–1677). Pantheism is the doctrine that, 'in some sense more than merely metaphorical, God is all there is or all is God'.[26] It is a paradigm that has persisted in the history of thought with remarkable tenacity.

Spinoza insisted that there could be by definition only one substance that possessed all attributes. God and nature are therefore but two names for one identical reality. Otherwise, God-and-world would be a greater totality than God alone. In other words, if we believe that God is greater in every way than anything else in existence, then the existence of God-plus-creation must be ruled out.

Pantheism has traditionally been rejected by orthodox Christian theologians because it is interpreted as removing the distinction between the creator and creation, making God impersonal, implying a purely inherent rather than transcendent deity, and excluding human and divine freedom.[27] Christian mystics are therefore more likely to interpret their mystical experiences as union or oneness with God, while maintaining a transcendent view of God. A sense of the unity of all things, however, is the most important and central characteristic shared by all mystics. Walter Stace, in his book *The Teachings of the Mystics*, concludes this to be true for Hindu, Buddhist, Taoist, Christian, Islamic, Jewish and non-religious mystics alike.

The most important, the central characteristic in which all *fully developed* mystical experiences agree, and which in the last analysis is definitive of them and serves to mark them off from other kinds of experiences, is that they involve the apprehension of an *ultimate nonsensuous unity in all things*, a oneness or a One to which neither the senses nor the reason can penetrate.[28]

Conceptions of oneness and holism can also be found in the philosophy of idealism, which arose in opposition to materialism. Whereas materialism rejects mind as a reality genuinely distinct from the physical, idealism rejects the physical world as something that can exist independently of the mind.[29]

Berkeley (1685–1753) argued that the only genuinely existing physical world is a system of images that have no independent existence apart from the many minds that make up the real content of the world. It is reported that when his famous contemporary Samuel Johnson heard of Berkeley's view, he exclaimed, 'I refute it thus!' and stubbed his toe on a large stone.[30]

Another version of idealism, called transcendental idealism, was propounded by Kant (1724–1804). Whilst for Berkeley the physical world did not necessarily exist, for Kant it certainly did exist, but only as a system of possible appearances for many minds. The fact that everything we come across in what we call the real world exists in space and time, is due to the construction of our minds necessitating a spatial and temporal framework for all our thinking. The spatial and temporal character of the physical world is not related to any independently existing phenomenon, but stems from our particular way of perceiving things.[31]

Bradley (1846–1924) espoused an absolute idealism, more extreme than the empirical idealism of Berkeley or the transcendental idealism of Kant. His ideas approach those of eastern mystics. Feeling, thought, and volition are, for Bradley, the only materials of existence. Anything else is deemed to be illusion. Each individual is viewed as a 'centre of experience', standing in relation to all other 'centres of experience', all of which form constituents of a vast cosmic consciousness, or Absolute. The Absolute experiences itself by creating the illusion of distinct 'centres'. Sprigge explains this aspect of Bradley's philosophy as follows:

> . . . the universe as a whole, that is, the Absolute, feels itself within each centre, and feeling itself therein gives itself the illusion that it is a separate being from itself feeling itself in another centre, an illusion, of course, corrected for it in its own total experience, and one which we, or it in us, can see through in moments of illumination.[32]

The idea of a universal mind, experiencing itself through itself, was also central to the philosophy of Hegel (1770–1831). The following passage is taken from *The Philosophy of Right*:

> The history of mind is its own act. Mind is only what it does, and its act is to make itself the object of its own consciousness. In history its act is to gain consciousness of itself as mind, to apprehend itself in its interpretation of itself to itself . . . All actions, including world-historical actions, culminate with individuals as subjects giving actuality to the substantial. They are the living instruments of what is in substance the deed of the world mind and they are therefore directly at one with that deed though it is concealed from them and is not their aim and object.[33]

The philosophies of Schopenhauer (1788–1860) and Nietzsche (1844–1900) also contain the notion of a universal mind or spirit, although their focus is more on a universal will than on a universal mind. The parallels between Schopenhauer's 'Cosmic Will' and the concept of 'Brahman', or the Absolute Unity, in eastern religion, are particularly striking.[34] Schopenhauer's ideas were later embraced, to some extent, by Carl Jung in his theories of 'individuation' (self-fulfilment of one's own nature as it is related to the whole) and the 'collective unconscious'.[35]

In pre-twentieth century science, we find Kepler comparing the universe to a living organism, with the sun as its heart, and Newton making reference to the omnipresent God, in whom all things are contained and moved. William James also talks of a 'World-soul', and expresses the need for a theory or system of belief that goes beyond fragmentation.

> It is undeniably true that materialistic, or so-called 'scientific', conceptions of the universe have so far gratified the purely intellectual interests more than mere sentimental conceptions have. But, on the other hand, as already remarked, they leave the emotional and active interests cold. *The perfect object of belief would be a God or 'Soul of the World', represented both optimistically and moralistically (if such a combination could be), and withal so definitely conceived as to show us why our phenomenal experiences should be sent to us by Him in just the very way in which they come.* All Science and all History would thus be accounted for in the deepest and simplest fashion . . . It is safe to say that, if ever such a system is satisfactorily excogitated, mankind will drop all other systems and cling to that one alone as real. Meanwhile the other systems coexist with the attempts at that one, and, all being alike fragmentary, each has its little audience and day.[36]

I believe that such a system is now coming together from the various holistic conceptions of the world, and from twentieth-century developments in science. Although the general trend of the past 2,500 years has taken us from a dominant perspective of right-brain holism and synthesis to one of left-brain reductionism and analysis, it can be argued that we are moving back to the old view of the world (albeit at a higher level of consciousness). We began by drawing no distinction between religious, philosophical and scientific ideas; what have for hundreds of years been considered three distinct areas may be coming together again (if they were ever truly apart) in a new cosmological consciousness.

> Like the waters of a river
> That in the swift flow of the stream
> A great rock divides,
> Though our ways seem to have parted
> I know that in the end we shall meet.
> (twelfth-century Japanese verse[37])

Some evidence for this view may be found in developments arising from the New Age movement.

THE NEW AGE

I have already mentioned the *New Physics* and the *New Psychology* (see Chapter 1). 'New' or 'holistic' approaches are also emerging in many other areas of science.[38] Indeed, the key adjectives of the past decade or so appear to be 'new' and 'holistic'.

According to a growing number of writers, we are at the dawning of a new era.[39] This new era is characterized by its holistic theme. The old institutions and ideologies, it is said, are crumbling to make way for the new.[40] We are being urged to abandon our old ways of thinking (involving reductionism, materialism, competition and conflict), and to consider new ways (involving holism, spirituality, co-operation, and harmony). We are being encouraged to give up our narrow perspectives and to widen our field of vision, so that we might see the interconnectedness of all things.

This holistic philosophy can be seen in the latest scientific thinking[41]; the growing importance attached to 'green' issues in politics; the increasing influence of eastern religions in western philosophical thinking; the growth of 'alternative' medicine and 'alternative' lifestyles[42]; the introduction of systems theories in a wide range of disciplines[43]; and the emergence and subsequent growth of humanistic and transpersonal psychologies.[44]

In 1991 a *Channel Four* television series on the New Age movement was screened. It brought forty prominent New Age thinkers together to discuss the various approaches and philosophies that form part of the movement. In the book that emerged from the programme, the editor William Bloom attempts to draw the threads together. He identifies four major areas where the New Age influence is strongly evident.[45]

First, there is the area of *New Paradigm/New Science*, under which he places all the new theories involved in changing our understanding of life and the world we inhabit. These include the New Physics of Quantum Theory and Relativity, and some of the latest developments in chemistry and biology.[46] The new Chaos Theory in mathematics could also be included with its underlying philosophy of interconnectedness.[47] The link between all these developments is their move away from reductionist to holistic thinking, leading some writers to talk in terms of a 'paradigm shift' or scientific revolution.[48]

Secondly, the concept of interdependence is extended to *Ecology*, particularly through the Green movement and the Gaia hypothesis.[49] The latter refers to James Lovelock's view of the Earth as a living, self-regulating organism (called 'Gaia' after the Greek Earth goddess). Our world is a living body, of which we form an integral part. We are like cells in a 'planetary body'.[50] This is an idea that has been taken even further by some cosmologists, who declare the universe to be 'one vast mind'[51] or 'a vast continuum of creative mind and intelligence'.[52] The central philosophy is this – 'Everything is affected by everything'.[53]

Thirdly, the *New Psychology* adds a further dimension with its humanistic and transpersonal focus (see Chapter 2). The 'alternative' or so-called 'holistic' approaches to medicine would be included in this area, as would a variety of psychotherapeutic techniques.[54] Once again, the theme is one of interconnectedness – between mind, body and spirit, and between individual, social system and environment.

Fourthly, Bloom identifies the area of *Spiritual Dynamics* as 'the hallmark of the New Age'. The spiritual influence, he argues, has been held down by the weights of repression, fear, power interests and materialism. These weights are now being lifted and 'the slumbering spiritual mammoth, like Gulliver released from the many strands, is beginning to awake'.[55] The influence of religion and mysticism comes across very strongly in Transpersonal Psychology,[56] and it is certainly evident in recent coverage of the New Physics.[57] All of which leads Sir George Trevelyan, founder of the British New Age movement, to talk in terms of a 'spiritual awakening in our time'.[58]

As Ra Bonewitz argues, 'everything is part of everything else – nothing is separate'.[59] There is an increasing sense of the interconnectedness and fundamental unity in all things. The Hegelian *zeitgeist* ('spirit of the times'[60]) is manifesting itself in a new wave of human consciousness – a higher level of consciousness, that is certainly holistic and perhaps even mystical.

We are, indeed, surrounded by evidence in support of the idea that we are entering a 'new age' of interconnectedness. Improved transport and communication links have contributed to a 'smaller world', where we do not seem to be as far apart from each other as we used to be. Journeys that used to take months can now be carried out in hours. Titbits of information from around the globe that were once relayed to a select few by word of mouth, or by letter, are now replaced by the barrage of information conveyed to the masses through the media of television, newspapers, and so on. As a result, we are becoming more aware of our neighbours and their problems.

Currently we are experiencing a coming together of the European nations. We have also recently witnessed what most people would have considered impossible only a few years ago – the removal of the Berlin Wall. The establishment of a McDonald's burger bar in Moscow may not rank alongside such a major event, but it is further evidence of a breaking down of barriers that at one time seemed insurmountable. The growing number of 'feed the world' charity drives is further evidence that something is happening. There is a heightened awareness, induced in no small part by the media and advanced technological communication networks. Certainly, if this new consciousness continues to grow, and if enough people adopt the New Age philosophy of holism and harmony, then a united world could become a real possibility.

Alvin Toffler, in his book *The Third Wave*, concludes that 'a new civilization is forming', and that we are presently experiencing the break-up of the old 'Second Wave' civilization, which is now in a state of crisis.[61] Crisis, he argues, is a necessary catalyst for change.[62] The old systems must enter into a state of crisis before breaking up to make way for the new.

Toffler's three 'waves' of change are the agricultural revolution, the industrial revolution, and the next revolution, the beginnings of which we are now witnessing. I have attempted to capture the essence of his thesis in the following extracts:

We are the children of the next transformation, the Third Wave . . . Humanity faces a quantum leap forward. It faces the deepest social upheaval and creative restructuring of all time. Without clearly recognizing it, we are engaged in building a remarkable new civilization from the ground up . . . The First Wave of change – the agricultural revolution – took thousands of years to play itself out. The Second Wave – the rise of the industrial civilization – took a mere three hundred years. Today history is even more accelerative, and it is likely that the Third Wave will sweep across history and complete itself in a few decades . . . This new civilization, as it challenges the old, will topple bureaucracies, reduce the role of the nation-state, and give rise to semi-autonomous economies in a post-imperialist world. It requires governments that are simpler, more effective, yet more democratic than any we know today . . . Third Wave people, meanwhile, will adopt new assumptions about nature, progress, evolution, time, space, matter, and causation. Their thinking will be less influenced by analogies based on the machine, more shaped by concepts like process, feedback, and disequilibrium . . . A host of new religions, new conceptions of science, new images of human nature, new forms of art will arise – in far richer diversity than was possible or necessary during the industrial age . . . Third Wave civilization . . . makes allowance for individual difference, and embraces (rather than suppresses) racial, regional, religious, and subcultural variety.[63]

While the holistic philosophy of the New Age movement may sometimes fall short of what could be described as mystical consciousness (some of it fails to go beyond the 'whole person', and is therefore very much grounded in self consciousness), the movement away from reductionist thinking towards notions of unity and interconnectedness suggests that we are currently undergoing a shift in human consciousness. F.C. Happold described this shift in consciousness over a quarter of a century ago:

> Something is happening in the world. The human race has packed up its tents and is once more on the march. Political, social and economic institutions, secular and religious thought-patterns and attitudes, are in the melting pot. The old foundations have been shaken, the old images shattered, the old models have proved inadequate. The new spiritual wine cannot be contained in the old conceptual bottles . . . we are in the midst of one of those evolutionary mental and spiritual 'leaps' which have happened before in history . . . what we see happening around us is an enlargement of human consciousness, a widening of perception and a natural growth in the collective soul of mankind.[64]

This enlargement of human consciousness is seen by some as part of the evolutionary process. If this is so, then the New Age that we are witnessing now may simply be the beginning of the next evolutionary stage. Humanity may currently be in a state of transition, between self and mystical consciousness.

CONSCIOUS EVOLUTION

In 1873, a Canadian psychologist, Richard Maurice Bucke, had a sudden and illuminating metaphysical experience that changed his life. Writing in the third person, he describes the experience as follows:

> He and two friends had spent the evening reading Wordsworth, Shelley, Keats, Browning, and especially Whitman. They parted at midnight, and he had a long drive in a hansom (it was in an English city). His mind deeply under the influence of the ideas, images and emotions called up by the reading and talk of the evening, was calm and peaceful. He was in a state of quiet, almost passive enjoyment. All at once, without warning of any kind, he found himself wrapped around as it were by a flame colored cloud. For an instant he thought of fire, some sudden conflagration in the great city, the next he knew that the light was within himself. Directly afterwards came upon him a sense of exaltation, of immense joyousness accompanied or immediately followed by an intellectual illumination quite impossible to describe. Into his brain streamed one momentary lightning-flash of the Brahmic Splendor which has ever since lightened his life; upon his heart fell one drop of Brahmic Bliss, leaving thenceforward for always an after taste of heaven. Among other things he did not come to believe, he saw and knew that the Cosmos is not dead matter but a living Presence, that the soul of man is immortal, that the universe is so built and ordered that without any peradventure all things work together for the good of each and all, that the foundation principle of the world is what we call love and that the happiness of every one is in the long run

absolutely certain. He claims that he learned more within a few seconds during which the illumination lasted than in previous months or even years of study, and that he learned much that no study could ever have taught.[65]

Years later, he developed a theory that not only explained his own experience, but also embraced all forms of mystical experience and divine revelation (including that received and passed on to us by the prophets). This theory was first published in 1901 in Richard Bucke's book *Cosmic Consciousness*. I present it here as a 'high-level' theory of religion and mystical experience that is somewhat compatible with the Bahá'í concept of progressive revelation, with New Age thinking generally and, more specifically, with my own 'theory of theories' (see Chapter 4).

'Cosmic consciousness' is what Richard Bucke believed he had experienced. There are, Bucke argues, three distinct forms of consciousness. The first of these is *simple consciousness*. This is possessed by all higher animals, such as dogs or horses, which are conscious of the things around them. At one time in our evolutionary history, it was the only form of consciousness we possessed. Some time around 300,000 years ago, we developed a second form of consciousness – *self consciousness* – a faculty that allowed us to become conscious of ourselves as distinct entities apart from the rest of the universe. Upon this 'master faculty', which raised us to a level above the animals, we were able to build a superstructure of language, reason, customs, industries and arts. The third form of consciousness has only recently (in terms of the scale of evolution) begun to emerge. It is the level of *cosmic consciousness* – a level of consciousness as far removed from self consciousness as the latter is from simple consciousness. So far, this higher level of consciousness has only been exhibited by the great religious prophets and a small number of mystics. Cosmic consciousness may be described as the highest form of mystical experience. It is no less than *God consciousness* (involving a sense of communion with God or with some greater whole), sometimes called 'Christ consciousness', 'Brahmic consciousness' or 'enlightenment'. Bucke describes it as follows:

> The prime characteristic of cosmic consciousness is, as its name implies, a consciousness of the cosmos, that is, of the life and order of the universe . . . Along with the consciousness of the cosmos there occurs an intellectual enlightenment or illumination which alone would place the individual on a new plane of existence – would make him almost a member of a new species . . . The person who passes through this experience will learn in the few minutes, or even moments, of its continuance more than in months or years of study, and he will learn much that no study ever taught or can teach. Especially does he obtain such a conception of THE WHOLE, or at least of an immense WHOLE, as dwarfs all conception, imagination or speculation, springing from and belonging to ordinary self consciousness, such a conception as makes the old attempts to mentally grasp the universe and its meaning petty and even ridiculous.[66]

While not everybody would agree with certain aspects of Richard Bucke's thesis, I feel that his basic argument is of interest. The notion that it is not just our bodies that evolve, but also our minds, does not seem unreasonable (we do, after all, inherit mental as well as physical characteristics). It is an idea that was reinforced, just over thirty years ago, by the famous Jesuit priest and palaeontologist, Father Pierre Teilhard de Chardin.

Teilhard de Chardin devoted more than fifty years of his life to the disciplines of geology, mammalian palaeontology and anthropology. His contribution to science was recognized by Unesco in 1965, when they held an international colloquium to commemorate the tenth anniversary of his death and that of Albert Einstein (they died in the same country within eight days of one another). The central theme of his magnum opus, *The Phenomenon of Man*, was evolutionism – not just biological, but extended to take in consciousness.[67]

He viewed the universe as an evolutionary process, always moving towards greater complexity and higher levels of consciousness. The process has been marked by a few dramatic leaps, notably the emergence of life on earth and the development of rational self consciousness in the human species. As a result of the latter, evolution is no longer subject to the laws of nature alone – we have a hand in directing it. In the fulfilment of this process, all things will be gathered up in God.[68]

According to the Teilhardian thesis, each successive stage in the evolutionary process is marked, first, by an increasing degree of complexity in organization and, second, by a corresponding increase in degree of consciousness. Evolution proceeds in orderly fashion from the inorganic to the organic, from less complex to more highly complex organized forms of life, through the process of 'hominization' and beyond to 'planetization', whereby all of humanity will collectively achieve an ultrahuman convergence, seen symbolically as a final 'Point Omega'.[69]

The universe, Teilhard argues, in its surge onwards and upwards towards higher forms of consciousness, branched out ceaselessly in different forms. Once the animal level was reached, the index of fuller consciousness became *cephalization*, a more intricate and highly developed nervous system.

In this steady upward thrusting, the line of development in primates became radial, leading to the advent of humanity.

With the establishment of the human species on earth, evolution, according to Teilhard, passed a critical threshold – the threshold of reflection. Human awareness of awareness brought with it inventiveness, creativity, foresight, planning, and freedom, with its concomitant responsibility, and the power to love or refuse love. Evolution was moving into the self-conscious stage, after several wrong turnings, or at least incomplete successes – the pre-hominids and neanderthaloids. The arrival and spread of *homo sapiens* brought with it another phenomenon – that element in the hominization process known as *socialization*.

Teilhard noted that certain forms of socialization – the organized clustering of individuals within a group, with differentiation of function for the common good – are observable in life other than human. However, on the subhuman level, socialization is always characterized by a certain mechanization, as typified in the ant hill or beehive. It lacks the qualities present in reflection – spontaneity, inventiveness, foresight, freedom and love.

The growth of the human population and technological advancement, particularly in the areas of transport and communication, are central factors involved in bringing about a common consciousness, or shared human awareness. Teilhard is optimistic about the future of humanity, provided we choose the right option – positive commitment to a convergent, yet differentiating personal communion. In other words, each person should develop his or her individual uniqueness to the full in the process of universal convergence.[70]

This notion of 'unity in diversity' is also central to the Bahá'í Faith. It is expressed by 'Abdu'l-Bahá as follows:

Consider the flowers of a garden, though differing in kind, colour, form and shape, yet, inasmuch as they are refreshed by the waters of one spring, revived by the breath of one wind, invigorated by the rays of one sun, this diversity increaseth their charm and addeth to their beauty. How unpleasing to the eye if all the flowers and plants, the leaves and blossoms, the fruits, the branches and the trees of that garden were all of the same shape and colour! Diversity of hues, form and shape, enricheth and adorneth the garden, and heighteneth the effect thereof. In like manner, when divers shades of thought, temperament and character, are brought together under the power and influence of one central agency, the beauty and glory of human perfection will be revealed and made manifest.[71]

Bahá'u'lláh proclaimed that the oneness of humanity would be achieved in the next stage of social evolution. A new world state, representing the consummation of human evolution, would emerge after periods of upheaval and chaos. The different stages in the evolutionary development of the species are regarded as being similar to the stages in the life of an individual.[72]

Our present state of crisis may thus be likened to the turbulent period of an adolescent prior to the attainment of adulthood.[73] Rejection of authority (as in the turning away from religion and the church), openness to experimentation (as in the relaxation of moral standards and the current experimentation with 'alternative living'), and internal struggle (as in increased social and psychological malaise) are all manifestations of our 'adolescent crisis'.

Psychologist and author Peter Russell, in his view of evolution, also follows much the same line as Teilhard. We are, he believes, moving towards a 'fifth level of evolution',[74] having evolved from primordial energy to matter to organic life and, most recently, to our present state of human consciousness. The fifth level will be the collective human consciousness or planetary consciousness that Teilhard predicted would arise from the mental convergence of humanity.

Russell likens our position to that of 'cells' in a 'global brain'. Just as atoms evolved into cells, cells into life, and life into human consciousness, human consciousness may well evolve into a global consciousness. He notes that there are approximately 10^{10} atoms in a living cell; 10^{10} cells in a human brain; a potentially stable human population of 10^{10} brains; and an estimated 10^{10} other planets in our galaxy capable of supporting life. He suggests that this number may represent an organizational critical mass that marks the threshold of quantum leaps in evolution.

Interestingly enough, there are also an estimated 10^{10} stars in our galaxy; an estimated 10^{10} galaxies in our universe; and our universe is now somewhere around 10^{10} years old. The next leap may not be too far away. The world's population is expected to reach 10^{10} in fifty or sixty years' time.[75]

Given the present exponential growth rate of technological and communications development, approximately half a century should be enough time to prepare the way for what promises to be the greatest moment in history since the emergence of human consciousness. It is perhaps no coincidence that communications experts are now using the human brain as a model for the development of communications systems for the future. Individuals and nations are literally being linked together in the same way that our brain cells are linked.

There certainly seems to be growing support for a view of human development such as Richard Bucke's theory of cosmic consciousness. Bucke's concept, however, goes further than most theories of conscious evolution. It accords well with the highly respected Teilhardian thesis, and it adds to this a means of understanding some important processes underlying mystical experience.

If we believe that humanity has evolved from a state of simple consciousness, surely it seems reasonable to believe that this process will continue and that mystical consciousness (or cosmic consciousness, in Bucke's terms) will be the next stage in our evolutionary journey. We appear to have what Arthur Koestler calls an 'integrative tendency',[76] which is pulling us more closely together and in the general direction of mystical consciousness. This tendency has sometimes been referred to as the 'love of God' or the 'divine spark'.[77] Added to this is the divine revelation passed to us by the prophets to help us on our way.

It would appear that, quite literally, all things will eventually be gathered up in God.

ULTIMATE
ANSWERS

This book, and the ten years of research that went into it, represents a quest – a quest for understanding and meaning. I have gained a lot from the experience. I began my search for truth as an agnostic, believing that all the answers would be revealed through science. I am now totally convinced that the answers lie outside science, but that science has a role to play in validating those answers.

In this final chapter, I will attempt to bring various threads together in a synthesis of psychology, physics and religion. I offer this synthesis to all seekers after a theory of everything; it is a theory of *almost* everything.

A THEORY OF ALMOST EVERYTHING

A child is born into a world of ever-changing forms. It begins life with a simple level of consciousness, and the information passed on by its parents at conception is encoded at an unconscious level. Building on this foundation, parents, guardians and teachers contribute to the growth of a higher level of consciousness. Distinctions are drawn between forms, and concepts such as 'I', 'me' and 'mine' are introduced.[1]

Eventually, a fully developed self consciousness emerges from the process of maturation and education. The self becomes the centre of the universe, and everything else is viewed in relation to it.

For some of these children, the self remains the centre of the universe throughout their adulthood and until they die. Their consciousness does not expand sufficiently to allow them to glimpse the truth. Their view of the world is analogous to Aristotle's view of a stationary earth, around which everything else orbits.[2] Others, more fortunate in adulthood, eventually accept a view of the self that is more like the Copernican model of astronomy, with the self just one of many selves orbiting around a much more important centre. This higher level of consciousness is God-centred.

Just as parents and teachers provide the child with conceptual frameworks (beliefs, attitudes, values, rules, and so on) to promote the growth of self consciousness, the building blocks for the next level of consciousness are offered by the prophets. Many adults listen for the message that will take them to this higher level, but they fail to hear it because of the clamour of dogma and symbol that has built up around it. Others, having acquired the ability to think for themselves, are too proud to listen to anything other than the sound of their own voices.

For those who earnestly strive for complete understanding, however, the limits of self consciousness are eventually transcended. The illusion of separateness evaporates and is replaced by an overwhelming impression of unity; despair turns to hope; anger to compassion; suffering to joy; and feelings of meaninglessness are replaced by a sense of meaning and understanding. This is the mystical experience towards which the prophets of religion seek to guide us.

The story is one of transition – from the hell of the 'selfish universe' and its reflection, the 'physical universe', to the heaven of the 'mystical universe'. I began with the search for meaning and understanding in the 'selfish universe' – a world where such a search may be likened to a hand trying to grasp itself; where life has lost all meaning; where the self has been enthroned in the place of God; and where the self exists only to serve the self.

The 'physical universe' offers no more hope than the 'selfish universe'. One is merely a reflection of the other. Both are based on the illusion of separateness. The world 'out there' is viewed as something that exists to serve the world 'within'. Again, the quest for meaning and understanding is doomed to circularity.

Only in the 'mystical universe' do we find what we are looking for. Understanding and meaning are revealed through communion with God in the mystical experience – an experience to which we are led by following the teachings and examples of the prophets.

In the same way that the child's consciousness matures towards an increasing state of preparedness for self consciousness, the human species is evolving towards an increasing state of preparedness for mystical consciousness. The prophets are the educators of the species just as parents and teachers are the educators of the individual. We are being pushed and pulled simultaneously towards the next stage of our development by the forces of conscious evolution and divine revelation. As our consciousness expands, more is revealed to us.

The latest signs from science and the New Age movement are that we are beginning to make the transition to this next stage. The old 'universes' are beginning to crumble. The illusion of separateness is under threat from the spirit of holism. Scientists no longer see the cosmos as a collection of independent objects each made up of something akin to minute billiard balls. Space, time, matter and energy are no longer viewed as independent concepts.

The importance of mind is now also recognized in evaluating our observations. Depending on what we choose to look at, the world may take on a form that can be understood in terms of either particles or waves. It may also be viewed in terms of continuously changing patterns of energy, with some patterns recurring and changing slowly to give the impression of solid objects that we refer to as matter. Space and time are merely concepts that we have invented to enable us to describe this change. Through these concepts, we relate different observations of change, or motion, to each other (the change from birth to death, for example, may be related to approximately seventy orbits around the sun). It should not surprise us too much, therefore, to discover that time and space are ultimately indistinguishable from one another.

My own theory of space–time–mind attempts to link the five concepts of space, time, mind, matter and energy, suggesting that they are, in fact, merely different physical (or mental) manifestations of the same substance. This blend of physics and psychology, however, still fails to provide the much-sought-after theory of everything. In attempting to take science to its current limits, we are left with a position of extreme relativism – everything is relative to everything else. That is the only absolute that appears to fit all the observations. In relation to our search for understanding and meaning, this, of course, takes us nowhere. Understanding and meaning are determined by one's position on the space–time–mind continuum (everything is relative to this position), but this leaves us with an infinity of truths and an infinity of meanings from which to choose. Nothing is right or wrong and nothing is good or bad in the context of extreme relativism.

Science is simply a rational approach to establishing relationships between various observations. As such, it can offer only relative truths. In order to progress from this position, it must always borrow at least one absolute truth from outside its own system. This takes us into the realm of religion and mysticism, where truth is revealed through communion with God, or mystical consciousness. It is this level of consciousness that scientists are now moving towards. Their pursuit of truth has pushed them beyond the limits of their own self consciousness. They have knocked hard on the doors of understanding and the doors are beginning to open. One such scientist is Paul Davies:

> In the end a rational explanation for the world in the sense of a closed and complete system of logical truths is almost certainly impossible. We are barred from ultimate knowledge, from ultimate explanation, by the very rules of reasoning that prompt us to seek an explanation in the first place. If we wish to progress beyond, we have to embrace a different concept of 'understanding' from that of rational explanation. Possibly the mystical path is a way to such an understanding. I have never had a mystical experience myself, but I keep an open mind about the value of such experiences. Maybe they provide the only route beyond the limits to which science and philosophy can take us, the only possible path to the Ultimate.[3]

I am convinced that mystical consciousness is 'the only route beyond the limits to which science and philosophy can take us' and 'the only possible path to the Ultimate'. I am also convinced that it is about to become the dominant mode of thinking. Before this can happen, however, many more individuals must follow the mystic way to escape from the prison of self. They may find their own way through earnest striving for truth, as many mystics, philosophers and scientists have done in the past, or they may simply follow the light of the prophets. But first, they must recognize that they are imprisoned. That is where this book (and others like it) can, perhaps, serve some purpose.

In summary, the main points I have tried to make are as follows:

● Human progress is facilitated by two things (both manifestations of the one source of Creation): the continuous expansion of consciousness (the 'push' factor); and progressive divine revelation (the 'pull' factor).

● Human consciousness has evolved from a simple 'animal' level (involving perceptions only) to a level of self consciousness (involving the linking of perceptions into concepts, which are all related to a central concept of self), and continues to evolve towards a mystical level (involving the linking of concepts into intuitions, which enable communion with God through the removal of the obstacle of the central concept of self).

● As our consciousness evolves towards an increasing state of preparedness to receive communion with God, more of the Absolute Truth is revealed to us through God's messengers.

● We are now very close to the next quantum leap in our evolutionary development; the old systems born out of self consciousness are showing signs of crumbling, and the illusion of separateness is giving way to perceptions of interconnectedness and unity. The beginnings of the new era are becoming increasingly apparent.

- This new age will be characterized by its holistic spirit. It will be based on religion (the Word of God as revealed through the prophets), but will rely heavily on a combination of religion and science to guide its development in the early stages. When mystical consciousness has been fully developed, rational thinking will be superseded by a new high-level intuition.

- The 'theory of everything' sought by scientists is an impossible dream; no system based on rational thinking alone can ever be complete. Progress in this area can only be achieved by science and religion working together. This will help to take us into the new era.

- A synthesis of ideas from psychology and physics is offered in a seven-dimensional space–time–mind conception of reality as the nearest that science can presently come to complete understanding. This approach leaves us in a position of extreme relativism with no absolutes to guide us. Science can offer only relative truths; absolute truth can only be found in the mystical core of religion, as revealed by the prophets. Science must move forward by testing the message of the prophets against its methods, and in doing so, it will help religion to move forward.

- All major religions contain one essential message: we must give up our attachment to the self in order to fulfil our destiny (which involves total communion and perfect harmony with God). If we put ourselves first, we will be last.

- If we follow the wisdom of the prophets, we will enter a state of mystical consciousness (communion with God) and will gain access to the Mind of God, according to our own conceptions.

THE MEANING OF LIFE

> When one is released from the prison of self, that is indeed freedom! For self is the greatest prison.
> —'*Abdu'l-Bahá*[4]

> To live for self is the source of all misery.
> — *Paramahansa Yogananda*[5]

Look beyond the self that you see in the looking glass of the world, and the universe will reveal itself to you in all its beauty. The self can best be served by giving up the self to love and to serve others.

This is the main message that emerges from *all* religions – detachment as the road to advancement. We need to give up attachment to the self and attachment to the material world. In effect, we need to give up the self in order to fulfil the self. Self-fulfilment lies in service to the whole or to God, not in service to the illusory little self that we have created.

Locked within the prison of self, we lose all sense of meaning, because there is no reason outside the self for our existence. The self exists only to serve the self. As Ecclesiastes discovered, meaninglessness is all that one finds when seeking to glorify the self. Is it not, therefore, likely that we will find meaning when seeking to glorify that which extends beyond the self?

Meaning is all about relationship. The meaning of human life is ultimately derived from its relationship with God. Thus the meaning of life for each of us will vary according to our personal relationship with God. The more we serve God through our actions, the more we commune with God through our consciousness, the more we know God and feel His presence, the more we 'become the image and likeness of God',[7] the greater the meaning our lives will take on.

Ultimately, we are left with the choice between self consciousness and God consciousness, the 'selfish universe' or the 'mystical universe'. One involves the material world, egotism, and a sense of separateness; the other, a spiritual existence, selflessness, and a sense of integrity. One appears to give rise to a great deal of conflict and suffering on both the individual and collective levels; the other, it is claimed, peace and happiness. We are all familiar with the former, but most of us know little or nothing about the latter.

In evolutionary terms, we are mere adolescents. Our present identity crisis prevents us from seeing the true beauty of the world. If, like the prodigal son, we return to our Father and make our peace with Him, we will see the beauty of the world, we will experience the oneness of all things, we will cease our futile search in the desert of the self, and our lives will take on meaning.

Notes

Reference details are listed alphabetically in the bibliography.

INTRODUCTION
1. Encyclopaedia Britannica, Hutchins & Adler, 1952a, p.vi

CHAPTER ONE
1. Gleick, 1988, p.23
2. Spinoza, 1677 (Encyclopaedia Britannica, Hutchins & Adler, 1952b, p.371)
3. Encyclopaedia Britannica, Hutchins & Adler, 1952c, p.290
4. Piaget, 1954
5. See Burns, 1979 on the development of the concept of self
6. See Claxton, 1981
7. Forer, 1949
8. Rosenthal, 1968
9. Ferguson, 1982
10. Lynch, 1988, p.75
11. Schachter, 1964
12. James, 1890 (Encyclopaedia Britannica, Hutchins & Adler, 1952a, p.200)
13. Barnaby, 1988
14. Rabbani, 1975
15. Kushner, 1987
16. Huddleston, 1980, p.11
17. Ibid., p.12
18. Birch, 1971

CHAPTER TWO
1. Stace, 1960, pp.33–4
2. Hawking, 1988
3. Hawking, 1988; Gribbin, 1987
4. Weinberg, 1983
5. Encyclopaedia Britannica, Goetz, 1986
6. Hawking, 1988
7. Bucke, 1989
8. Frankfort et al., 1949
9. Encyclopaedia Britannica, Goetz, 1986
10. Gregory, 1981
11. See Hawking, 1988
12. Khursheed, 1987
13. Ibid.
14. Claxton, 1981, p.28
15. Watson, 1913
16. Greening, 1988
17. Association for Humanistic Psychology, 1987, p.8
18. Rowan, 1988
19. Association for Humanistic Psychology, 1987, p.4
20. Maslow, 1968
21. Rogers, 1961
22. Association for Humanistic Psychology, 1987, p.10
23. Graham, 1986
24. Rowan, 1988
25. Graham, 1986
26. Reason & Rowan, 1981
27. Graham, 1986
28. Steiner, 1960
29. Hunt, 1980, p.71
30. Sire, 1977, p.198
31. Campbell, 1984
32. Perls, 1976
33. Gardner, 1983, pp.301–3
34. Ibid., p.303–4

35. Claxton, 1981, pp.74–5
36. Graham, 1986
37. Happold, 1966
38. Ibid.
39. Encyclopaedia Britannica, Goetz, 1986
40. Happold, 1966
41. Ibid., pp.28–9
42. Huddleston, 1980, pp.22–3
43. Ibid., p.23
44. Kushner, 1990
45. Khursheed, 1987, p.1
46. Adler, 1992, p.12
47. Central Statistical Office, 1991
48. Jung, 1964, p.94

CHAPTER THREE
1. Encyclopaedia Britannica, Hutchins & Adler, 1952c, p.297
2. Pascal, 1670 (quoted in Gross, 1983, p.229)
3. Walsh & Vaughan, 1980
4. Abbott, 1974, p.3
5. Lynch, 1988
6. Schumacher, 1978
7. Ibid., p.50
8. Quoted in Schumacher, 1978, p.52
9. Schumacher, 1978, p.55
10. Honner, 1987
11. Hofstadter, 1980, pp.408–9
12. Gribbin, 1987
13. Herbert, 1985
14. Gribbin, 1987
15. Polkinghorne, 1988
16. Gribbin, 1985
17. Casti, 1989
18. Ibid.
19. Gribbin, 1987
20. Pagels, 1983
21. Polkinghorne, 1988
22. Pagels, 1983
23. Ibid., p.190
24. Quoted in Hoffman, 1973, pp.247–8
25. Gardner, 1976
26. Zukav, 1984
27. Pagels, 1983

28. Gardner, 1976
29. Zukav, 1984
30. Gardner, 1976, p.8
31. Ibid., p.10
32. Epstein, 1985
33. Hawking, 1988
34. Gribbin, 1987
35. Zukav, 1984
36. Gribbin, 1987
37. Zukav, 1984
38. Einstein & Infeld, 1938
39. Taubes, 1983
40. Barrow, 1988
41. Davies, 1989
42. Taubes, 1983
43. Davies, 1989
44. Ibid.
45. Hawking, 1988
46. See Weinberg, 1983; Weisskopf, 1983; Contopoulos & Kotsakis, 1987; or Gribbin, 1987 on the origin of the universe

CHAPTER FOUR
1. Cooley, 1902
2. Ibid.
3. Burns, 1979
4. Markus & Smith, 1981
5. Kuiper & Derry, 1981
6. Lewicki, 1984
7. Greenwald, 1980
8. Cooley, 1902
9. Barry, 1990
10. Ibid.
11. Ibid.
12. Graham, 1990
13. Calder, 1982
14. Gregory, 1981, p.536
15. Kuhn, 1962
16. Schumacher, 1978
17. Birch, 1971
18. Wilber, 1979
19. Doise, 1986

CHAPTER FIVE
1. Quoted in Weber, 1986, p.8
2. Quoted in Pais, 1982, p.319
3. 'Abdu'l-Bahá, 1979, p.143

4. Gregory, 1981
5. See Hofstadter, 1980
6. Gregory, 1981
7. Davies, 1992
8. Ibid., p.167
9. Bronowski, 1977
10. Penrose, 1989
11. Bronowski, 1977, pp.60–61
12. Khursheed, 1987
13. Ibid., p.1
14. Gribbin, 1987
15. Jung, 1964
16. Encyclopaedia Britannica, Goetz, 1986
17. Gotlib & Colby, 1987
18. See Dossey, 1982; Graham, 1990
19. Graham, 1990
20. See Graham, 1990; Ferguson, 1982; Westland, 1978; Kline, 1988
21. See Ferguson, 1982; Toffler, 1981
22. Toffler, 1981, p.135
23. See Lord Northbourne, 1963 on this analogy
24. Ward, 1991, p.vii
25. Ibid.
26. 'Abdu'l-Bahá, 1979, p.141
27. Capra, 1983
28. Khursheed, 1987, p.52
29. Ibid., p.53
30. Huddleston, 1980
31. Davies, 1992, pp.229–30
32. Bahá'u'lláh, quoted in Hofman, 1960, p.53
33. Huddleston, 1980
34. Parrinder, 1964, p.27
35. Rohani, 1991
36. Ibid., p.10
37. Encyclopaedia Britannica Yearbook, Daume, 1986
38. Basham, 1977
39. Rohani, 1991
40. Parrinder, 1964
41. Encyclopaedia Britannica, Goetz, 1986
42. See especially Capra, 1983

43. Rohani, 1991
44. Werblowsky, 1977
45. For example, Ferguson, 1978
46. For example, Encyclopaedia Britannica, Goetz, 1986
47. See Davies, 1992 on this point
48. Buddhist Publishing Group, 1985
49. See Capra, 1983; Zukav, 1984
50. Quoted in Hart-Davis, 1983
51. Hooper, 1979
52. Lewis, 1979, p.79
53. Ibid., pp.83–4
54. Koran, 1972
55. Peale, 1983
56. Stone, 1975
57. Birch, 1971
58. Fromm, 1950
59. Ali, 1951
60. Parrinder, 1964
61. Bahá'u'lláh, 1952, p.216
62. 'Abdu'l-Bahá, 1979, pp.130, 142
63. Hofman, 1960, pp.61–2
64. National Bahá'í Center Public Information Office, 1976
65. Bahá'u'lláh, 1978, p.220
66. National Bahá'í Center Public Information Office, 1976
67. Quoted in Hofman, 1960, pp.55–6
68. Khursheed, 1987
69. Toynbee, 1956
70. Quoted in Murphy, 1980, p.518
71. Davies, 1989, p.203

CHAPTER SIX

1. See Capra, 1983; Zukav, 1984
2. Stace, 1960
3. Happold, 1970
4. Ibid.
5. See, for example, Wilson, 1987 on meditation techniques
6. Parrinder, 1964
7. See Jacobi, 1944 on Jung
8. Toynbee, 1956
9. Happold, 1970, p.121
10. Ibid., p.58
11. Goldsmith, 1986, pp.178–9

12. Bahá'u'lláh, 1992
13. Ibid., p.48
14. 'Abdu'l-Bahá, 1982, p.148
15. Genesis 1:26
16. Happold, 1966, p.119
17. Happold, 1970
18. Spencer, 1963
19. Plato, c. 347 BC (Encyclopaedia Britannica, Hutchins & Adler, 1952e, p.767)
20. Spencer, 1963
21. Ibid.
22. Encyclopaedia Britannica, Goetz, 1986
23. Encyclopaedia Britannica, Hutchins & Adler, 1952c, p.267
24. Steiner, 1960
25. Encyclopaedia Britannica, Goetz, 1986
26. Meagher et al, 1979
27. Encyclopaedia Britannica, Goetz, 1986
28. Stace, 1960, pp.14–15
29. Sprigge, 1985
30. Hawking, 1988
31. Sprigge, 1985
32. Ibid., p.70
33. Encyclopaedia Britannica, Hutchins & Adler, 1952e, pp.110–11
34. Sprigge, 1985
35. See Fordham, 1966 on Jung
36. James, 1890 (Encyclopaedia Britannica, Hutchins & Adler, 1952a, pp.658–9)
37. Quoted in Barrow, 1988
38. See Graham, 1990; Ferguson, 1982; Harvey, 1986
39. For example, Bloom, 1991; Ferguson, 1982; Harvey, 1986; Toffler, 1981
40. Ferguson, 1982; Harvey, 1986; Toffler, 1981
41. See Davies, 1989 on the resurgence of holism
42. See Graham, 1990; Harvey, 1986
43. Laszlo, 1972
44. See Graham, 1986; Rowan, 1988; Walsh & Vaughan, 1980
45. Bloom, 1991
46. See especially Zukav, 1984 (on physics); Prigogine & Stengers, 1984 (on chemistry); and Rose, Lewontin & Kamin, 1984 (on biology). See also Bohm, 1980; Sheldrake, 1981; Capra, 1983; Peat, 1987; Augros & Staneiu, 1987; Davies, 1989; Casti, 1989.
47. See Gleick, 1988 on Chaos Theory
48. See, for example, Kuhn, 1962; Ferguson, 1982; Graham, 1986
49. Lovelock, 1979
50. An analogy used by Russell, 1982; Hubbard, 1983; Watson, 1987
51. Foster, 1975
52. Trevelyan, 1983
53. Schul, 1978
54. See Harvey, 1986; Graham, 1990
55. Bloom, 1991, p.xvii
56. See Walsh & Vaughan, 1980
57. See Capra, 1983; Zukav, 1984; Davies, 1989
58. Trevelyan, 1977
59. Bonewitz, 1988
60. A concept introduced by Hegel in his *The Phenomenology of Spirit* in 1807 (Encyclopaedia Britannica, Hutchins & Adler, 1952d)
61. Toffler, 1981
62. See also Ferguson, 1982 on this point
63. Toffler, 1981, pp.23, 24, 134, 268, 366
64. Happold, 1966, p.177
65. Bucke, 1989 (first published 1901), pp.7–8
66. Ibid., pp.2, 61
67. De Chardin, 1959
68. O'Sullivan, 1981
69. Glick, 1976
70. Grau, 1976
71. Quoted in Huddleston, 1980,

p.60

72. Laszlo, 1989
73. Khursheed, 1987
74. Russell, 1982
75. Encyclopaedia Britannica Yearbook, Daume, 1986
76. Koestler, 1972
77. Happold, 1970

CHAPTER SEVEN

1. See Claxton, 1981
2. See Hawking, 1988
3. Davies, 1992, pp.231–2
4. Quoted in Paine, 1944, p.70
5. Yogananda, 1988, p.113
6. 'Abdu'l-Bahá, 1982, p.451

BIBLIOGRAPHY

Abbott, E.A. (1974) *Flatland: A Romance of Many Dimensions*. Oxford: Basil Blackwell.

'Abdu'l-Bahá (1979) *Paris Talks*. London: Bahá'í Publishing Trust.

— (1982) *Promulgation of Universal Peace*. Wilmette, Illinois: Bahá'í Publishing Trust.

Adler, A. (1992) *What Life Could Mean to You*. Oxford: Oneworld.

Ali, Maulana Muhammad (1951) *The Holy Qur'án*. Lahore: Ahmadiyya Anjuman Isha'at Islam.

Association for Humanistic Psychology (1987) *The Meaning of Humanistic Psychology*. San Francisco: AHP.

Augros, R. & Staneiu, G. (1987) *The New Biology: Discovering the Wisdom in Nature*. Boston and London: New Science Library.

Bahá'u'lláh (1952) *Gleanings from the Writings of Bahá'u'lláh* (trans. Shoghi Effendi). Wilmette, Illinois: Bahá'í Publishing Trust.

— (1978) *Tablets of Bahá'u'lláh* (trans. Habib Taherzadeh et al.). Haifa, Israel: Bahá'í World Centre.

— (1992) *The Seven Valleys of Bahá'u'lláh* (trans. Ali-Kuli Khan). Oxford: Oneworld.

Barnaby, F. (1988) *The Gaia Peace Atlas*. London: Pan Books.

Barrow, J.D. (1988) *The World within the World*. Oxford: Clarendon Press.

Barry, R. (1990) *Self and Other Perception: A Holistic Framework*. Unpublished PhD Thesis. School of Psychology, Queen's University, Belfast.

Basham, A.L. (1977) Hinduism. In R.C. Zaehner (Ed.) *The Concise Encyclopaedia of Living Faiths*. London: Hutchinson.

Birch, C. (1971) 'Purpose in the universe: A search for wholeness'. *Zygon: Journal of Religion and Science*. March 1971, pp.4–15.

Bloom, W. (1991) *The New Age: An Anthology of Essential Writings*. London: Rider.

Bohm, D. (1980) *Wholeness and the Implicate Order*. London: Routledge & Kegan Paul.

Bonewitz, R. (1988) *The Pulse of Life*. Longmead, Dorset: Element Books.

Bronowski, J. (1977) *A Sense of the Future: Essays in Natural Philosophy*. (Selected and edited works by P.E. Ariotti). Cambridge, Mass.: MIT Press.

Bucke, R.M. (1989) *Cosmic Consciousness: A Study in the Evolution of the Human Mind*. New Jersey: Citadel.

Buddhist Publishing Group (1985) *Buddhism*. Leicester: Buddhist Publishing Group.

Burns, R.B. (1979) *The Self Concept: Theory, Measurement, Development and Behaviour*. New York: Longman.

Calder, N. (1982) *Einstein's Universe*. Harmondsworth, Middlesex: Penguin.

Campbell, E. (1984) 'The end of innocence'. *Journal of Humanistic Psychology*, 24 (No. 2), 6–29.

Capra, F. (1983) *The Tao of Physics*. London: Flamingo.

Casti, J.L. (1989) *Paradigms Lost: Images of Man in the Mirror of Science*. London: Cardinal.

Central Statistical Office (1991) *1991 – 50 Years of the CSO*. Statistical fact sheet to commemorate the 50th anniversary of the CSO. London: HMSO.

Claxton, G. (1981) *Wholly Human: Western and Eastern Visions of the Self and its Perfection*. London: Routledge & Kegan Paul.

Contopoulos, G. & Kotsakis, D. (1987) *Cosmology: The Structure and Evolution of the Universe*. Berlin: Springer-Verlag.

Cooley, C.H. (1902) *Human Nature and the Social Order*. New York: Scribners.

Coy, G. (1979) *Counsels of Perfection: A Bahá'í Guide to Mature Living*. Oxford: George Ronald.

Daume, D.D. (Ed.) (1986) *1986 Britannica Book of the Year*. Chicago: Encyclopaedia Britannica.

Davies, P. (1989) *The Cosmic Blueprint*. New York: Touchstone.

— (1992) *The Mind of God: Science and the Search for Ultimate Meaning*. London: Simon & Schuster.

De Chardin, Pierre Teilhard (1959) *The Phenomenon of Man*. London: Collins.

Doise, W. (1986) *Levels of Explanation in Social Psychology*. Cambridge: Cambridge University Press.

Dossey, L. (1982) *Space, Time & Medicine*. Boulder, Colorado: Shambhala.

Einstein, A. & Infeld, L. (1938) 'The Evolution of Physics'. *Gateway to the Great Books*, Vol. 8. Chicago: Encyclopaedia Britannica.

Epstein, L.C. (1985) *Relativity Visualized*. San Francisco: Insight Press.

Ferguson, J. (1978) *Religions of the World: A Study for Everyman*. Guildford and London: Lutterworth Educational.

Ferguson, M. (1982) *The Aquarian Conspiracy: Personal and Social Transformation in the 1980s*. London: Paladin.

Fordham, F. (1966) *An Introduction to Jung's Psychology*. Harmondsworth, Middlesex: Penguin.

Forer, B.R. (1949) 'The Fallacy of Personal Validation: A Classroom Demonstration of Gullibility'. *Journal of Abnormal and Social Psychology*, Vol. 44.

Foster, D. (1975) *The Intelligent Universe*. London: Abelard.

Frankfort, H., Frankfort, H.A., Wilson, J.A. & Jacobsen, T. (1949) *Before Philosophy*. Harmondsworth, Middlesex: Penguin.

Fromm, E. (1950) *Psychoanalysis and Religion*. New Haven, USA: Yale

University Press.

Gardner, M. (1976) *The Relativity Explosion*. New York: Vintage Books.

— (1983) *Science Good, Bad and Bogus*. Oxford: Oxford University Press.

Gleick, J. (1988) *Chaos*. London: Cardinal.

Glick, T.F. (1976) Pierre Teilhard de Chardin. In C.C. Gillespie (Ed.) *Dictionary of Scientific Biography*, Volume 13. New York: Charles Scribner's Sons.

Goetz, P.W. (Ed.) (1986) *The New Encyclopaedia Britannica*, Volumes 1–29. Chicago: Encyclopaedia Britannica.

Goldsmith, J.S. (1986) *A Parenthesis in Eternity*. New York: Harper & Row.

Gotlib, I.H. & Colby, C.A. (1987) *Treatment of Depression: An Interpersonal Systems Approach*. New York: Pergamon Press.

Graham, H. (1986) *The Human Face of Psychology*. Milton Keynes: Open University Press.

— (1990) *Time, Energy, and the Psychology of Healing*. London: Jessica Kingsley.

Grau, J.A. (1976) *Morality and the Human Future in the Thought of Teilhard de Chardin*. Cranbury, New Jersey: Associated University Press.

Greening, T. (1988) 'Commentary by the Editor'. *Journal of Humanistic Psychology*, 28 (No. 4), 68–72.

Greenwald, A.G. (1980) 'The totalitarian ego: Fabrication and revision of personal history'. *American Psychologist*, 35, 603–18.

Gregory, R.L. (1981) *Mind in Science*. London: Weidenfeld and Nicolson.

Gribbin, J. (1985) *In Search of Schrodinger's Cat*. London: Corgi Books.

— (1987) *In Search of the Big Bang*. London: Corgi Books.

Gross, J. (1983) *The Oxford Book of Aphorisms*. Oxford: Oxford University Press.

Happold, F.C. (1966) *Religious Faith and Twentieth-Century Man*. Harmondsworth, Middlesex: Penguin.

— (1970) *Mysticism: A Study and an Anthology*. Harmondsworth, Middlesex: Penguin.

Hart-Davis, R. (1983) *A Beggar in Purple*. London: Hamish Hamilton.

Harvey, D. (1986) *Thorsons Complete Guide to Alternative Living*. Wellingborough: Thorsons Publishing Group.

Hawking, S.W. (1988) *A Brief History of Time*. London: Bantam Press.

Herbert, N. (1985) *Quantum Reality: Beyond the New Physics*. New York: Anchor Press.

Hoffman, B. (1973) *Albert Einstein, Creator and Rebel*. New York: Viking Press.

Hofman, D. (1960) *The Renewal of Civilization*. London: George Ronald.

Hofstadter, D.R. (1980) *Godel, Escher, Bach: An Eternal Golden Braid*. Harmondsworth, Middlesex: Penguin.

Honner, J. (1987) *The Description of Nature: Niels Bohr and the Philosophy of Quantum Physics*. Oxford: Clarendon Press.

Hooper, W. (1979) Preface to C.S. Lewis. *God in the Dock*. Glasgow: Fount.

Hubbard, Barbara Marx. (1983) *The Evolutionary Journey*. Wellingborough, Northants: Turnstone Press.

Huddleston, J. (1980) *The Earth is but One Country*. London: Bahá'í

Publishing Trust.

Hunt, D. (1980) *The Cult Explosion*. Eugene, Oregon: Harvest House.

Hutchins, R.M. & Adler, M. (Eds.) (1952a) *Great Books of the Western World*, Volume 53: William James, 'The Principles of Psychology'. Chicago: Encyclopaedia Britannica.

— (1952b) *Great Books of the Western World*, Volume 31: Benedict de Spinoza, 'Ethics'. Chicago: Encyclopaedia Britannica.

— (1952c) *Great Books of the Western World*, Volume 12: Marcus Aurelius, 'The Meditations of Marcus Aurelius'. Chicago: Encyclopaedia Britannica.

— (1952d) *Great Books of the Western World*, Volume 46: Hegel, 'The Philosophy of Right'. Chicago: Encyclopaedia Britannica.

— (1952e) *Great Books of the Western World*, Volume 7: Plato, 'Laws'. Chicago: Encyclopaedia Britannica.

Jacobi, J. (1944) *The Psychology of C.G. Jung*. London: Kegan Paul.

Jung, C.G. (1964) *Man and His Symbols*. New York: Doubleday.

Khursheed, A. (1987) *Science and Religion: Towards the Restoration of an Ancient Harmony*. London: Oneworld.

Kline, P. (1988) *Psychology Exposed or the Emperor's New Clothes*. London and New York: Routledge.

Koestler, A. (1972) *The Roots of Coincidence*. London: Hutchinson.

Koran, A. (1972) *Bring Out the Magic in Your Mind*. Wellingborough, Northants: Thorsons Publishing Group.

Kuhn, T.S. (1962) 'The structure of scientific revolutions'. *International Encyclopaedia of Unified Science 2*, 11. London and Chicago: University of Chicago Press.

Kuiper, N.A. & Derry, P.A. (1981) 'The self as a cognitive prototype: An application to person perception and depression'. In N. Cantor & J.F. Kihlstrom (Eds.) *Personality, Cognition, and Social Interaction*. Hillsdale, New Jersey: Lawrence Erlbaum Associates.

Kushner, H.S. (1987) *When All You've Ever Wanted Isn't Enough*. London: Pan Books.

— (1990) *Who Needs God*. London: Simon & Schuster.

Laszlo, E. (1972) *The Systems View of the World*. New York: Braziller.

— (1989) *The Inner Limits of Mankind: Heretical Reflections on Today's Values, Culture and Politics*. London: Oneworld.

Lewicki, P. (1984) 'Self-schema and social information processing'. *Journal of Personality and Social Psychology*, 47, 1177–90.

Lewis, C.S. (1979) *God in the Dock*. Glasgow: Fount.

Lovelock, J.E. (1979) *Gaia*. London: Oxford University Press.

Lynch, J. (1988) *Living Beyond Limits: The Tao of Self-Empowerment*. Walpole, New Hampshire: Stillpoint Publishing.

Markus, H. & Smith, J. (1981) 'The influence of self-schemata on the perception of others'. In N. Cantor & J.F. Kihlstrom (Eds.) *Personality, Cognition, and Social Interaction*. Hillsdale, New Jersey: Lawrence Erlbaum Associates.

Maslow, A.H. (1968) *Toward a Psychology of Being*. New York: Van Nostrand.

Bibliography

Meagher, P.K. et al. (1979) *Encyclopedic Dictionary of Religion* (Volume O–Z). Washington DC: Corpus Publications (Extract from p. 2659 in Britannica Research Paper R-8965).

Murphy, E.F. (1980) *The Macmillan Treasury of Relevant Quotations*. London: Macmillan Press.

National Bahá'í Center Public Information Office (1976) *Bahá'í Faith Fact Sheet*. Wilmette, Illinois: National Bahá'í Center Public Information Office.

Northbourne, Lord (1963) *Religion in the Modern World*. London: Dent & Sons.

O'Sullivan, T. (1981) Pierre Teilhard de Chardin. In J. Wintle (Ed.) *Makers of Modern Culture*. London: Routledge & Kegan Paul.

Pagels, H.R. (1983) *The Cosmic Code: Quantum Physics as the Language of Nature*. London: Michael Joseph.

Paine, M.H. (1944) *The Divine Art of Living*. Wilmette, Illinois: Bahá'í Publishing Trust.

Pais, A. (1982) *'Subtle is the Lord ...': The Science and the Life of Albert Einstein*. New York: Oxford University Press.

Parrinder, G. (1964) *The World's Living Religions*. London: Pan Books.

Peale, N.V. (1983) *The Power of Positive Thinking*. Tadworth, Surrey: Cedar Books.

Peat, F.D. (1987) *Synchronicity: The Bridge Between Matter and Mind*. New York: Bantam Books.

Penrose, R. (1989) *The Emperor's New Mind*. New York: Vintage Books.

Perls, F.S. (1976) *The Gestalt Approach and Eye Witness to Therapy*. New York: Bantam Books.

Piaget, J. (1954) *The Construction of Reality in the Child*. New York: Basic Books.

Polkinghorne, J.C. (1988) *The Quantum World*. London: Penguin.

Prigogine, I. & Stengers, I. (1984) *Order Out of Chaos: Man's New Dialogue with Nature*. London: Heinemann.

Rabbani, R. (1975) *Prescription for Living*. Oxford: George Ronald.

Reason, P. & Rowan, J. (1981) *Human Inquiry: A Sourcebook of New Paradigm Research*. New York: Wiley.

Rogers, C.R. (1961) *On Becoming a Person: A Therapist's View of Psychotherapy*. London: Constable.

Rohani, M.K. (1991) *Accents of God: Selections from the World's Sacred Scriptures*. Oxford: Oneworld.

Rose, S., Lewontin, R.C. & Kamin, L.J. (1984) *Not In Our Genes: Biology, Ideology and Human Nature*. Harmondsworth, Middlesex: Penguin.

Rosenthal, R. (1968) 'Self-Fulfilling Prophecy'. *Psychology Today*, September 1968.

Rowan, J. (1988) *Ordinary Ecstasy: Humanistic Psychology in Action*. London: Routledge.

Russell, P. (1982) *The Awakening Earth*. London: Routledge & Kegan Paul.

Schachter, S. (1964) 'The interaction of cognitive and physiological determinants of emotional state'. In L. Berkowitz (Ed.) *Advances in Experimental Social Psychology* (Vol. 1). New York: Academic Press.

Schul, B. (1978) *The Psychic Frontiers of Medicine*. London: Coronet.

Schumacher, E.F. (1978) *A Guide for the Perplexed*. London: Abacus.

Sheldrake, R. (1981) *A New Science of Life*. London: Blond & Briggs.

Shook, G.A. (1974) *Mysticism, Science & Revelation*. Oxford: George Ronald.

Sire, J.W. (1977) *The Universe Next Door: A Guide to World Views*. Leicester: Inter-Varsity Press.

Spencer, S. (1963) *Mysticism in World Religion*. Harmondsworth, Middlesex: Penguin.

Sprigge, T.L.S. (1985) *Theories of Existence*. Harmondsworth, Middlesex: Penguin.

Stace, W.T. (1960) *The Teachings of the Mystics*. New York: Mentor.

Steiner, R. (1960) *Eleven European Mystics*. New York: Rudolf Steiner Publications.

Stone, W.C. (1975) *The Success System That Never Fails*. Wellingborough, Northants: Thorsons Publishing Group.

Taubes, G. (1983) Einstein's Dream. *Discover*, December 1983.

Toffler, A. (1981) *The Third Wave*. London: Pan Books.

Toynbee, A. (1956) *An Historian's Approach to Religion*. London: Oxford University Press.

Trevelyan, G. (1977) *A Vision of the Aquarian Age*. London: Coventure.

— (1983) Preface to B.M. Hubbard. *The Evolutionary Journey*. Wellingborough, Northants: Turnstone Press.

Walsh, R.N. & Vaughan, F. (1980) *Beyond Ego: Transpersonal Dimensions in Psychology*. Los Angeles: Tarcher.

Ward, K. (1991) *A Vision to Pursue: Beyond the Crisis in Christianity*. London: SCM Press.

Watson, J.B. (1913) 'Psychology as the behaviorist views it'. *Psychological Review*, 20, 158–77.

Watson, L. (1987) *Supernature II*. London: Sceptre.

Weber, R. (1986) *Dialogues with Scientists and Sages: The Search for Unity*. London and New York: Routledge & Kegan Paul.

Weinberg, S. (1983) *The First Three Minutes*. London: Flamingo.

Weisskopf, V.F. (1983) 'The Origin of the Universe'. *American Scientist*, September–October 1983, 473–80.

Werblowsky, R.J.Z. (1977) 'Juadaism, or the religion of Israel'. In R.C. Zaehner (Ed.) *The Concise Encyclopaedia of Living Faiths*. London: Hutchinson.

Westland, G. (1978) *Current Crises of Psychology*. London: Heinemann.

Wilber, K. (1979) *The Spectrum of Consciousness*. Wheaton, Illinois: Theosophical Publishing House.

Wilson, P. (1987) *The Calm Technique: Simple Meditation Methods That Really Work*. Wellingborough, Northants: Thorsons Publishing Group.

Yogananda, P. (1988) *Where There is Light: Insight and Inspiration for Meeting Life's Challenges*. Los Angeles: Self-Realization Fellowship.

Zukav, G. (1984) *The Dancing Wu Li Masters: An Overview of The New Physics*. London: Flamingo.

INDEX